About This Book

Teaching problem solving just got easier! Your friends at *The Mailbox®* magazine have compiled a resource of 40 high-interest activities that will help students make sense of mathematics and become more confident problem solvers. The tasks in *POW! Problem of the Week Grades 5–6* are designed to give students practice with a variety of problem-solving strategies and lots of different math skills. The activities—20 at each grade level—progress from easy to more challenging, making it easy for you to best me_' students' needs.

This book provides brief descriptions of ten diff€ including sample problems and solutions.

In addition, there is a special two-page lesson on each strategy that you can use with the whole class to introduce or review that strategy. Each lesson consists of a teacher page and an accompanying student page that shows students step by step how to use the strategy.

Also included is a checklist of the problem-solving process that you can duplicate for students to keep in their folders, plus a handy generic rubric to help you with assessment.

Each of the 40 problem-solving activities consists of a colorful teacher page and a reproducible student page. The teacher page includes the following:

- the overall objective of the problem
- a list of problem-solving strategies students could use to solve the problem
- a list of math skills students will use to solve the problem
- a brief summary of the problem
- a list of important information found in the problem
- an answer key
- a bonus box key
- a list of helpful hints for the teacher to share with students when they need help solving the problem

The student reproducible includes the problem and explains what the student should do to solve it.

Turn to this resource whenever you want your students to have a meaningful problem-solving experience that helps them make sense of mathematics!

Table of Contents

How to Use This Book

POW! Problem of the Week Grades 5–6 makes teaching the problem-solving process easy. It provides everything you need: helpful background information, engaging teaching lessons, exciting student activities, and a handy assessment rubric! Use this great resource in the following ways:

- **Have students practice the important steps of the problem-solving process (page 5).** Give each student a copy of "Solving the Problem" to keep in a folder. It lists the five key steps in the problem-solving process: read it, think it, solve it, write it, and review it. Have students use the guide with each problem in the book.

- **Assess students' understanding of the problem-solving process (page 6).** Make a copy of the handy math rubric. Use it and students' written responses to help you assess their thinking during the problem-solving process and to check their understanding of each strategy.

- **Use the overview of ten problem-solving strategies as a reference (pages 7–11).** Refer to this handy guide for a brief description of and sample problem for each problem-solving strategy.

- **Introduce or review key problem-solving strategies (pages 12–31).** Teach students how to use and apply the problem-solving strategies with the ready-to-use lessons that follow the overview. For each lesson, make a transparency of the student reproducible, plus a copy for each student. Then just follow the directions on the colorful teacher page.

- **Make problem solving fun and exciting with high-interest problems (pages 32–111).** Select from activities that are arranged by grade level and progress in order from less to more challenging. Each activity consists of a page for the teacher and one for the student. Scan the teacher page to find the problem-solving strategies or math skills students need to practice. Read the problem summary and the important information found in the problem. Note that there are even hints to give students who get stuck while solving a problem! Remind students to refer to the steps listed on their "Solving the Problem" page. Use the problems in a variety of ways:

- independent practice or homework
- morning work or free-time activities
- partner or small-group practice
- weekly learning center activities
- whole-group instruction
- assessment

Solving the Problem

Complete each step below to help you solve the problem. On a separate sheet of notebook paper, write your responses to Steps 2–5.

1. Read It—Read the problem. Then reread the problem to reveal information not noticed during the first read.

2. Think It—Think about the problem. Then rewrite the problem to be solved in your own words. Next, list any information in the story that may help you solve the problem.

3. Solve It—Use the listed information to help you solve the problem. Show your work on a scrap piece of paper. Write the solution or answer to the problem using complete sentences.

4. Write It—Write a short summary of how you solved the problem. Include the problem-solving strategy or strategies you used and any charts, diagrams, or drawings you may have used. Describe which strategies worked and which ones didn't work. Also include whether you received help from another classmate or parent and tell how that person helped you.

5. Review It—Does your answer make sense? Is it reasonable? If you think you don't have the correct answer, explain why. Then describe where you got stuck or made an error. Tell about the most important or most interesting thing you learned from doing this problem.

Act It Out

Draw a Picture or Diagram

Make a List, Table, or Chart

Guess and Check

Find a Pattern

Write an Equation

Work Backward

MATH RUBRIC

4 Identifies all of the important parts of the problem

Fully understands the math needed to solve the problem

Communicates mathematical thinking clearly and creatively in written work

3 Identifies most of the important parts of the problem

Understands most of the math needed to solve the problem

Communicates mathematical thinking clearly in written work

2 Identifies some of the important parts of the problem

Understands some of the math needed to solve the problem

Communicates some mathematical thinking in written work

1 Identifies few of the important parts of the problem

Understands little of the math needed to solve the problem

Communicates little mathematical thinking in written work

Choose the Correct Operation

Solve a Simpler Problem

Logical Reasoning

Work Backward

Logical Reasoning

Solve a Simpler Problem

Choose the Correct Operation

Write an Equation

Find a Pattern

Guess and Check

Make a List, Table, or Chart

Draw a Picture or Diagram

Act It Out

Problem-Solving Strategies

Act It Out

The act-it-out strategy involves having problem solvers either role-play or physically manipulate objects, such as paper squares, to help them develop a visual image of the problem's data. The strategy is especially helpful when students need to visualize spatial relationships.

Sample problem: Six paper triangles—orange, red, yellow, green, blue, and purple—are arranged in two rows of three each. The orange triangle is to the right of the red triangle. The yellow triangle is between the green and blue triangles. The red triangle is above the blue triangle. How are the triangles arranged?

Solution: Top row: red, orange, purple
Bottom row: blue, yellow, green

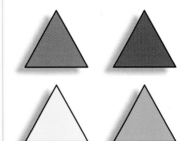

Draw a Picture or Diagram

Problem solvers use the draw-a-picture or draw-a-diagram strategy when they need to create a simple picture or diagram to help them visualize a problem. The strategy is especially helpful if a problem involves mapping.

Sample problem: Trevor left his campsite and hiked $4\frac{7}{8}$ miles south to the river. He then hiked $3\frac{1}{2}$ miles west to a cave. Then he turned north and hiked $3\frac{1}{4}$ miles to a deserted cabin. After he rests awhile, Trevor plans to hike east to pick up the first trail. When he leaves the cabin, how far does Trevor have to hike to reach the campsite?

Solution: The trail from the cabin to the first trail completes a rectangle, so it measures $3\frac{1}{2}$ miles. The distance from that point back to the campsite is $1\frac{5}{8}$ miles: $4\frac{7}{8}$ miles − $3\frac{1}{4}$ miles. The distance from the cabin to the campsite is $5\frac{1}{8}$ miles: $3\frac{1}{2}$ miles + $1\frac{5}{8}$ miles.

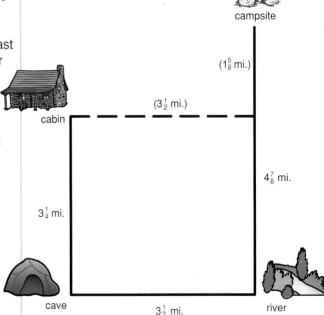

Problem-Solving Strategies

Make a List, Table, or Chart

The strategy of making a list, table, or chart is often used when the information in a problem needs to be organized. Such organizers help problem solvers keep track of or spot missing data. Students can also discover relationships and patterns among the data.

Sample problem: Boards on Wheels, Inc., is gearing up for its annual skateboarding competition. This year's contest will involve skateboarders from three different towns. For every eight skateboarders from Oakdale, there will be 12 skateboarders from Twin Oaks and nine skateboarders from Oakwood. If 72 skateboarders from Oakwood will be at the competition, how many skateboarders from each of the other two towns will be there?

Solution: Oakdale: 64, Twin Oaks: 96

Oakdale	8	16	24	32	40	48	56	64
Twin Oaks	12	24	36	48	60	72	84	96
Oakwood	9	18	27	36	45	54	63	72

Guess and Check

The guess-and-check strategy is used when problem solvers need to make a reasonable guess about the solution. After a guess has been made, it is checked and, if necessary, revised. Each subsequent guess helps make the next one more accurate. In this manner, problem solvers gradually get closer to the solution by making guesses that are increasingly more reasonable.

Sample problem: All together, 178 children attended Marcus's Magical Show. There were 44 more boys than girls who came. How many boys and how many girls attended the show?

Solution: 111 boys, 67 girls

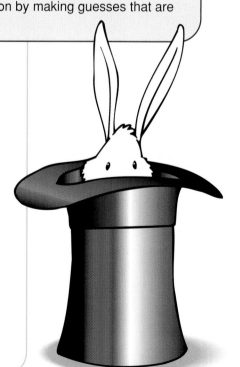

Problem-Solving Strategies

Find a Pattern

The find-a-pattern strategy is helpful when problem solvers have to analyze a numerical, visual, or behavioral pattern in data and then make a prediction or generalization based on that analysis. It may require problem solvers to extend a pattern or make a table to reveal a pattern.

Sample problem: Detective I. M. Stumped depends heavily on his dog, Sherlock, for help with his important cases. See if you can help this pair of sleuths crack the code to the pattern below. The solution contains at least one number and operation and must fit each set.

$$9 \underline{\hspace{1cm}} = 8$$
$$29 \underline{\hspace{1cm}} = 18$$
$$49 \underline{\hspace{1cm}} = 28$$
$$17 \underline{\hspace{1cm}} = \underline{\hspace{1cm}}$$

Solution:
$$(9 + 7) \div 2 = 8$$
$$(29 + 7) \div 2 = 18$$
$$(49 + 7) \div 2 = 28$$
$$(17 + 7) \div 2 = 12$$

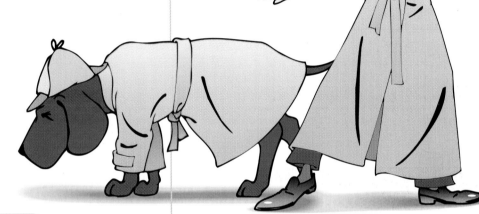

Work Backward

The work-backward strategy involves starting with the end result or data given at the end of a problem and making a series of inverse computations to find the missing information.

Sample problem: It is 6:00 P.M., and Granny Smith is still shopping at the mall. So far, she has spent 45 minutes browsing through magazines in a bookstore, 40 minutes listening to CDs in a music store, one hour dreaming about diamonds in a jewelry store, and 35 minutes trying on dresses in a department store. What time did she begin shopping?

Solution:
6:00 P.M. − 45 minutes = 5:15 P.M.
5:15 P.M. − 40 minutes = 4:35 P.M.
4:35 P.M. − 60 minutes = 3:35 P.M.
3:35 P.M. − 35 minutes = 3:00 P.M.

Problem-Solving Strategies

Logical Reasoning

The logical-reasoning strategy involves the use of conditional clues to help problem solvers arrive at a solution. Clues can be stated directly or implied. They can also be included in if-then statements. Displaying the data in a chart can help the problem solver work through the problem one statement at a time to arrive at the solution.

Sample problem: Five friends—Kelli, Kevin, Kurt, Karen, and Katie—met at Krazy Ken's Diner for lunch. But their waitress got confused and mixed up all the orders! Use the clues below to help sort out the orders. Put a √ in each box that is true and an X in each box that is not true.

Clues:
1. Kelli doesn't eat beef or pork.
2. Kevin did not order sausage.
3. Kurt prefers his meat sliced.
4. Karen did not order sausage or chopped beef.

Solution: Katie: sausage, Kevin: chopped beef, Kurt: sliced beef, Karen: ribs, Kelli: chicken

Sample problem:

	chopped beef	chicken	sliced beef	sausage	ribs
Katie					
Kevin					
Kurt					
Karen					
Kelli					

Solution:

	chopped beef	chicken	sliced beef	sausage	ribs
Katie	X	X	X	✓	X
Kevin	✓	X	X	X	X
Kurt	X	X	✓	X	X
Karen	X	X	X	X	✓
Kelli	X	✓	X	X	X

Write an Equation

Problem solvers use the write-an-equation strategy when they need to write a mathematical sentence to model information in a problem.

Sample problem: Alex spent $5.00 playing video games and bought two same-priced candy bars to eat as a snack. He spent a total of $9.00. How much did each candy bar cost?

Solution: Let c = the candy bar.
$$2 \times c + \$5.00 = \$9.00$$
$$2 \times c = \$4.00$$
$$c = \$2.00$$

Problem-Solving Strategies

Choose the Correct Operation

The choose-the-correct-operation strategy involves having problem solvers decide which mathematical operation to use: addition, subtraction, multiplication, or division. Identifying key words and phrases in a problem can suggest which operation is appropriate for solving a given problem.

Sample problem: Guests at a brunch ate four platters of cream-filled danish pastries. Each platter contained 20 pastries. If the guests also ate 75 fruit-filled pastries, how many pastries did they eat in all?

Solution: (4 x 20) + 75 = 155 pastries

Solve a Simpler Problem

The solve-a-simpler-problem strategy is used when a problem is too complex for problem solvers to solve in one step. A problem can be simplified by dividing it into smaller problems to solve, by substituting smaller numbers for larger numbers, or by decreasing the number of given items. The simpler representation can then reveal a pattern or suggest what operation or process to use to solve the problem.

Sample problem: Big Al, better known as Alligator Al, makes plastic alligators for Gator Land Theme Park. He sells one-half of his plastic gators and gives away one-fourth of the remaining ones. If he gave away 360 toy gators, how many did he have in the beginning?

Solution: 2,880 toy gators

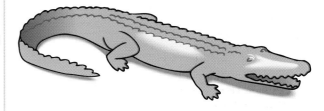

1. Since 36 x 10 = 360, use 36 for the number of toys given away.
2. Let g = the number of toys before any were given away.
   $1/4 \times g = 36$
   $g = 36 \times 4$
   $g = 144$
3. Let t = the original number of toys.
   $1/2 \times t = 144$
   $t = 144 \times 2$
   $t = 288$
4. Multiply to find the actual number of toys.
   $288 \times 10 = 2,880$

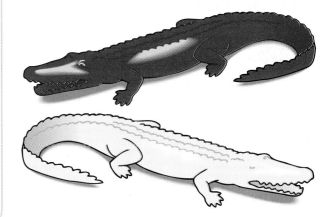

Lessons for Teaching Problem-Solving Strategies

Lesson 1: Act It Out

Description of strategy: The act-it-out strategy involves having problem solvers either role-play or physically manipulate objects, such as paper squares, to help them develop a visual image of the problem's data. The strategy is especially helpful when students need to visualize spatial relationships.

Directions: Cut out the squares at the bottom of the transparency. Then guide students to complete page 13 according to the instructions below.

Getting started: Have students read problem 1. Discuss the questions below one at a time, having students fill in the correct answers on their papers as you write them on the transparency.

- What are you to find out? *(where Hobo is sitting)*
- How many clowns are on the bus? *(5)*
- Where is Klarabell sitting? *(in the front seat)* Koko? *(behind Smiley but in front of Lulu)* Smiley? *(in front of Koko)* Lulu? *(behind Koko)*
- Is it hard to picture in your mind where all of the clowns are sitting? *(Yes, it is very confusing trying to remember where each clown sits in relation to the others.)*
- Would it help to label squares of paper representing the clowns and move them around, or have 5 people role-play the parts of the clowns? Why? *(Yes, using paper squares or having people actually sit in chairs would make it easier to see the clowns' seating arrangement.)*
- What problem-solving strategy could you use? *(act it out)*

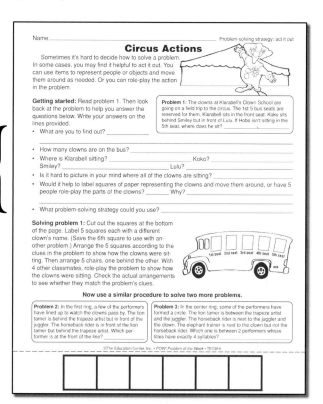

Solving problem 1: Have students cut out the squares at the bottom of the page and label them with the different clowns' names. Model how to look back at the clues and move the squares around to show how the clowns were seated. Then slowly read the problem aloud, having students verify that the arrangement is correct as shown.

Also have students role-play the problem's solution. Arrange five chairs in front of the room. Choose five volunteers to act out the clown's seating arrangement as you slowly read the problem aloud. Check to see that the arrangement is correct.

Solving problems 2 and 3: Guide students through a similar procedure to solve the problems together as a class. Or have students solve the problems independently. Direct students to reuse their cutouts by flipping them over or by erasing them and relabeling. *(2: trapeze artist, 3: juggler)*

Name_____ Problem-solving strategy: act it out

Circus Actions

Sometimes it's hard to decide how to solve a problem. In some cases, you may find it helpful to act it out. You can use items to represent people or objects and move them around as needed. Or you can role-play the action in the problem.

Getting started: Read problem 1. Then look back at the problem to help you answer the questions below. Write your answers on the lines provided.

- What are you to find out? _____

_____

- How many clowns are on the bus? _____
- Where is Klarabell sitting? _____ Koko? _____
Smiley? _____ Lulu? _____
- Is it hard to picture in your mind where all of the clowns are sitting? _____
- Would it help to label squares of paper representing the clowns and move them around, or have 5 people role-play the parts of the clowns? _____ Why? _____

_____

- What problem-solving strategy could you use? _____

Problem 1: The clowns at Klarabell's Clown School are going on a field trip to the circus. The 1st 5 bus seats are reserved for them. Klarabell sits in the front seat. Koko sits behind Smiley but in front of Lulu. If Hobo isn't sitting in the 5th seat, where does he sit? _____

Solving problem 1: Cut out the squares at the bottom of the page. Label 5 squares each with a different clown's name. (Save the 6th square to use with another problem.) Arrange the 5 squares according to the clues in the problem to show how the clowns were sitting. Then arrange 5 chairs, one behind the other. With 4 other classmates, role-play the problem to show how the clowns were sitting. Check the actual arrangements to see whether they match the problem's clues.

1st seat 2nd seat 3rd seat 4th seat 5th seat

Now use a similar procedure to solve two more problems.

Problem 2: In the first ring, a few of the performers have lined up to watch the clowns pass by. The lion tamer is behind the trapeze artist but in front of the juggler. The horseback rider is in front of the lion tamer but behind the trapeze artist. Which performer is at the front of the line? _____

Problem 3: In the center ring, some of the performers have formed a circle. The lion tamer is between the trapeze artist and the juggler. The horseback rider is next to the juggler and the clown. The elephant trainer is next to the clown but not the horseback rider. Which one is between 2 performers whose titles have exactly 4 syllables? _____

©The Education Center, Inc. • *POW! Problem of the Week* • TEC916

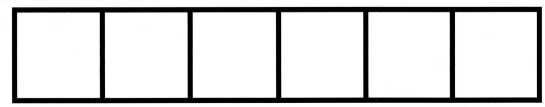

Note to the teacher: Each student will need scissors to complete this page.

13

Lessons for Teaching Problem-Solving Strategies

Lesson 2: Draw a Picture or Diagram

(**Description of strategy:**) Problem solvers use this strategy when a simple picture or diagram helps them visualize a problem. The strategy is especially helpful if a problem involves mapping.

(**Directions:**) Guide students to complete page 15 according to the instructions below.

(**Getting started:**) Have students read problem 1. Discuss the questions below one at a time, having students fill in the correct answers on their papers as you write them on the transparency.

- What are you to find out? *(3 things: the number of swimmers competing in all 3 events, the number competing in both the butterfly and backstroke but not the breaststroke, and the number competing in the backstroke only)*
- How many swimmers competed in both the breaststroke and the backstroke only? *(3)* The butterfly only? *(5)* The breaststroke only? *(6)* Both the breaststroke and butterfly, but not the backstroke? *(4)*
- How many total swimmers competed in the breaststroke? *(14)* The butterfly? *(17)* The backstroke? *(12)*
- Would it help to have a diagram that organizes the 3 groups of swimmers? Why? *(Yes, a diagram would help show which swimmers competed in each event.)*
- What problem-solving strategy could you use? *(draw a picture or diagram)*

Name _____ Problem-solving strategy: draw a picture or diagram

Picture This!
Drawing a picture or diagram is helpful in solving some types of math problems. Make drawings to help you solve each problem below.

Getting started: Read problem 1. Then look back at the problem to help you answer the questions below. Write your answers on the lines provided.

- What are you to find out? _____

- How many swimmers competed in both the breaststroke and backstroke only? _____ The butterfly only? _____ The breaststroke only? _____ Both the breaststroke and butterfly, but not the backstroke? _____

- How many total swimmers competed in the breaststroke? _____ The butterfly? _____ The backstroke? _____

- Would it help to have a diagram that organizes the 3 groups of swimmers? _____ Why? _____

- What problem-solving strategy could you use? _____

Problem 1: The Glendale Gators participated in a swim meet. Three swimmers competed in both the breaststroke and backstroke only. Five swimmers competed in the butterfly only. Six swimmers signed up to compete in the breaststroke only. Four swimmers competed in both the breaststroke and butterfly, but not the backstroke. Fourteen swimmers total competed in the breaststroke. Seventeen swimmers total competed in the butterfly. Twelve swimmers competed in all 3 events. _____ In both the butterfly and backstroke, but not the breaststroke? _____ In the backstroke only? _____

Solving problem 1: To help you organize the swimmers, use the Venn diagram shown. Reread the problem to find the number of swimmers competing in only 1 event. Write those numbers in the diagram where the circles do not intersect. Reread the problem to find the number of swimmers competing in only 2 events. Write those numbers in the diagram where 2 circles intersect. Finally, reread the problem to determine the numbers to write in the diagram's remaining blank sections so that the totals match the clues. Then check back over your work. Are your answers reasonable?

Now draw a picture or diagram to solve each problem below.

Problem 2: The swim meet was a great success! Fifteen ribbons were given on each level: 1st place, 2nd place, and 3rd place. Seven swimmers won 3rd-place ribbons only. No one won 3rd- and 2nd-place ribbons only. Four swimmers won both 1st- and 2nd-place ribbons only. Three swimmers won 1st- and 3rd-place ribbons only. How many swimmers won all 3 ribbons? _____ A 1st-place ribbon only? _____ A 2nd-place ribbon only?

Problem 3: After the swim meet, the Gators decided to take a relaxing walk. From the pool, the team walked 3 blocks north to the bank, then 2 blocks west to the hardware store. They continued by walking 5 blocks south, then 2 blocks east to an ice-cream shop. How far and in what direction does the team need to walk to get back to the pool?

©The Education Center, Inc. • POW! Problem of the Week • TEC916   15

Solving problem 1: Direct students to reread the problem to find the number of swimmers competing in only one event. Guide students to write those numbers in the diagram where no circles intersect. Repeat this process with the number of swimmers competing in only two events. Guide students to write those numbers in the diagram where two circles intersect. Have students read the problem again, this time writing numbers in the diagram's remaining blank sections to make the totals match the clues. Then have students check their work. *(One swimmer competed in all 3 events. Seven swimmers competed in both the butterfly and backstroke, but not the breaststroke. One swimmer competed in the backstroke only.)*

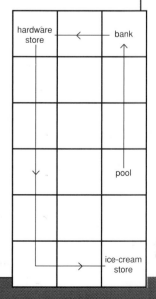

Breaststroke

6

4 3
1

5   7   1

Butterfly   Backstroke

Solving problems 2 and 3: Guide students through a similar procedure to solve the problems together as a class. Or have students solve the problems independently. For problem 2, direct students to draw another Venn diagram of three intersecting circles. For problem 3, have them draw a 3 x 6 grid. *(2: Five swimmers won all 3 ribbons. Three swimmers won 1st-place ribbons only. Six won 2nd-place ribbons only.)*

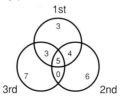

1st

3

3   4
5

7   0   6

3rd   2nd

(3: two blocks north)

hardware store	←	bank
		↑
↓		pool
	→	ice-cream store

Picture This!

Drawing a picture or diagram is helpful in solving some types of math problems. Make drawings to help you solve each problem below.

Getting started: Read problem 1. Then look back at the problem to help you answer the questions below. Write your answers on the lines provided.

- What are you to find out? _____

  _____

- How many swimmers competed in both the breaststroke and backstroke only? _____ The butterfly only? _____ The breaststroke only? _____ Both the breaststroke and butterfly, but not the backstroke? _____

Problem 1: The Glendale Gators participated in a swim meet. Three swimmers competed in both the breaststroke and backstroke only. Five swimmers competed in the butterfly only. Six swimmers signed up to compete in the breaststroke only. Four swimmers competed in both the breaststroke and butterfly, but not the backstroke. Fourteen swimmers total competed in the breaststroke. Seventeen swimmers total competed in the butterfly. Twelve swimmers total competed in the backstroke. How many swimmers competed in all 3 events? _____ In both the butterfly and backstroke, but not the breaststroke? _____ In the backstroke only? _____

- How many total swimmers competed in the breaststroke? _____ The butterfly? _____ The backstroke? _____

- Would it help to have a diagram that organizes the 3 groups of swimmers? _____ Why? _____

  _____

- What problem-solving strategy could you use? _____

Solving problem 1: To help you organize the swimmers, use the Venn diagram shown. Reread the problem to find the number of swimmers competing in only 1 event. Write those numbers in the diagram where the circles do not intersect. Reread the problem to find the number of swimmers competing in only 2 events. Write those numbers in the diagram where 2 circles intersect. Finally, reread the problem to determine the numbers to write in the diagram's remaining blank sections so that the totals match the clues. Then check back over your work. Are your answers reasonable?

Now draw a picture or diagram to solve each problem below.

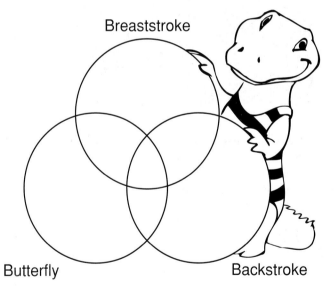

Breaststroke

Butterfly   Backstroke

Problem 2: The swim meet was a great success! Fifteen ribbons were given on each level: 1st place, 2nd place, and 3rd place. Seven swimmers won 3rd-place ribbons only. No one won 3rd- and 2nd-place ribbons only. Four swimmers won both 1st- and 2nd-place ribbons only. Three swimmers won 1st- and 3rd-place ribbons only. How many swimmers won all 3 ribbons? _____ A 1st-place ribbon only? _____ A 2nd-place ribbon only? _____

Problem 3: After the swim meet, the Gators decided to take a relaxing walk. From the pool, the team walked 3 blocks north to the bank, then 2 blocks west to the hardware store. They continued by walking 5 blocks south, then 2 blocks east to an ice-cream shop. How far and in what direction does the team need to walk to get back to the pool?

_____

Lesson 3: Make a List, Table, or Chart

(Description of strategy:) The strategy of making a list, table, or chart is often used when the information in a problem needs to be organized. Such organizers help problem solvers keep track of data, spot missing data, and discover relationships and patterns within data.

(Directions:) Guide students to complete page 17 according to the instructions below.

(Getting started:) Have students read problem 1. Discuss the questions below one at a time, having students fill in the correct answers on their papers as you write them on the transparency.

- What are you to find out? *(the number of different coin combinations that equal $0.55 using quarters, dimes, and/or nickels)*
- What snack does Marvin want to buy? *(a bag of popcorn)*
- How much does the popcorn cost? *($0.55)*
- What kinds of coins can he use? *(quarters, dimes, and/or nickels)*
- What is one possible combination Marvin can use? *(2 quarters and 1 nickel)*
- Are there more combinations Marvin can use? *(yes)* If so, how can you keep track of the different combinations? *(by making three columns: one for quarters, one for dimes, and one for nickels)*
- What problem-solving strategy can you use? *(making a list, table, or chart)*

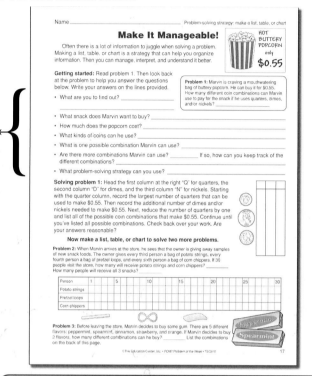

Solving problem 1: Have students head the three columns as directed. Next, have students list the largest number of quarters Marvin can use to make $0.55 *(2)*. Then help students determine the coins needed for the remaining cost of the popcorn *(0 dimes, 1 nickel)*. Next, have students reduce the number of quarters by one. Help them fill in the remaining columns to list all of the possible coin combinations using one quarter that make $0.55. In the same way, have students list all of the possible combinations using no quarters and then again using no dimes. Continue guiding students in this manner until all possible combinations have been listed. Have students check their work to see whether their answers are reasonable. *(11 combinations)*

Q	D	N
2	0	1
1	3	0
1	2	2
1	1	4
1	0	6
0	5	1
0	4	3
0	3	5
0	2	7
0	1	9
0	0	11

Solving problems 2 and 3: Guide students to solve the problems together as a class. Or have students solve the problems independently. For problem 2, have students use a table. For problem 3, have them make an organized list. *(2: 5 people, 2 people)*

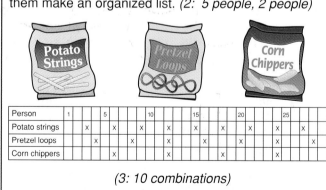

Person	1			5					10					15					20					25					30
Potato strings		X			X			X			X			X			X			X			X			X			X
Pretzel loops			X				X				X				X				X				X				X		
Corn chippers						X						X						X						X					X

(3: 10 combinations)

peppermint, spearmint   spearmint, cinnamon   cinnamon, strawberry
peppermint, cinnamon   spearmint, strawberry   cinnamon, orange
peppermint, strawberry   spearmint, orange
peppermint, orange   strawberry, orange

Make It Manageable!

HOT BUTTERY POPCORN only **$0.55**

Often there is a lot of information to juggle when solving a problem. Making a list, table, or chart is a strategy that can help you organize information. Then you can manage, interpret, and understand it better.

Getting started: Read problem 1. Then look back at the problem to help you answer the questions below. Write your answers on the lines provided.

Problem 1: Marvin is craving a mouthwatering bag of buttery popcorn. He can buy it for $0.55. How many different coin combinations can Marvin use to pay for the snack if he uses quarters, dimes, and/or nickels? _____

- What are you to find out? _____
  _____

- What snack does Marvin want to buy? _____

- How much does the popcorn cost? _____

- What kinds of coins can he use? _____

- What is one possible combination Marvin can use? _____

- Are there more combinations Marvin can use? _____ If so, how can you keep track of the different combinations? _____

- What problem-solving strategy can you use? _____

Solving problem 1: Head the first column at the right "Q" for quarters, the second column "D" for dimes, and the third column "N" for nickels. Starting with the quarter column, record the largest number of quarters that can be used to make $0.55. Then record the additional number of dimes and/or nickels needed to make $0.55. Next, reduce the number of quarters by one and list all of the possible coin combinations that make $0.55. Continue until you've listed all possible combinations. Check back over your work. Are your answers reasonable?

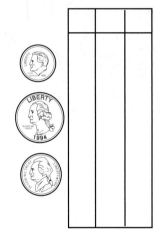

Now make a list, table, or chart to solve two more problems.

Problem 2: When Marvin arrives at the store, he sees that the owner is giving away samples of new snack foods. The owner gives every third person a bag of potato strings, every fourth person a bag of pretzel loops, and every sixth person a bag of corn chippers. If 30 people visit the store, how many will receive potato strings and corn chippers? _____ How many people will receive all 3 snacks? _____

Person	1				5					10					15					20					25					30
Potato strings																														
Pretzel loops																														
Corn chippers																														

Problem 3: Before leaving the store, Marvin decides to buy some gum. There are 5 different flavors: peppermint, spearmint, cinnamon, strawberry, and orange. If Marvin decides to buy 2 flavors, how many different combinations can he buy? _____ List the combinations on the back of this page.

Lessons for Teaching Problem-Solving Strategies

Lesson 4: Guess and Check

Description of strategy: The guess-and-check strategy is used when problem solvers need to make a reasonable guess about the solution. After the guess has been made, it is checked and, if necessary, revised. Each subsequent guess helps make the next one more accurate. In this manner, problem solvers gradually get closer to the solution by making guesses that are increasingly more reasonable.

Directions: Guide students to complete page 19 according to the instructions below.

Getting started: Have students read problem 1. Discuss the questions below one at a time, having students fill in the correct answers on their papers as you write them on the transparency.

- What are you to find out? *(the number of customers each friend checked out at the grocery store)*
- Who are the cashiers? *(Charlie, Chuck, Chrissy, and Cherie)*
- How many customers did Charlie help? *(twice as many as Chuck)* Chrissy? *(3 times as many as Chuck)* Cherie? *(2 less than 3 times as many as Chuck)*
- How many customers did the 4 cashiers help all together? *(97)*
- Would guessing an answer help you solve the problem? *(Yes, because there is not much information given.)*
- If your guess is wrong, can it still help you solve the problem? *(Yes, just make the next guess higher or lower, depending on the first guess.)*
- What problem-solving strategy can you use? *(guess and check)*

Solving problem 1: Ask students which cashier would be the best one to begin with and why. *(Chuck, because the least information is known about him, and what is known about everyone else is based on the number of Chuck's customers.)* Have students make a guess, such as 15, and use it to figure out the number of customers helped by the other cashiers: Charlie—30, Chrissy—45, Cherie—43. Next, have them check the guess by finding the total number of customers helped and comparing it to 97. Since 133 is greater than 97, have students guess a number less than 15, such as ten, and repeat the steps to check. Since this total *(88)* is too low, have students guess a number higher than ten but less than 15. Have students continue guessing and checking in this manner until the problem is solved. Then have students reread the problem and review their work to see whether their answers are reasonable. *(Chuck helped 11 customers; Charlie helped 22; Chrissy helped 33; and Cherie helped 31.)*

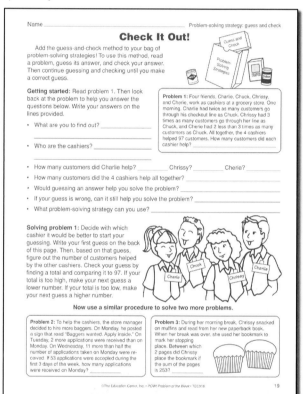

Solving problems 2 and 3: Guide students through a similar procedure to solve the problems together as a class. Or have students solve the problems independently. *(2: Monday—16, Tuesday—18, Wednesday—19; 3: pages 126 and 127)*

Check It Out!

Add the guess-and-check method to your bag of problem-solving strategies! To use this method, read a problem, guess its answer, and check your answer. Then continue guessing and checking until you make a correct guess.

Getting started: Read problem 1. Then look back at the problem to help you answer the questions below. Write your answers on the lines provided.

Problem 1: Four friends, Charlie, Chuck, Chrissy, and Cherie, work as cashiers at a grocery store. One morning, Charlie had twice as many customers go through his checkout line as Chuck. Chrissy had 3 times as many customers go through her line as Chuck, and Cherie had 2 less than 3 times as many customers as Chuck. All together, the 4 cashiers helped 97 customers. How many customers did each cashier help? _____

- What are you to find out? _____

  _____

- Who are the cashiers? _____

  _____

- How many customers did Charlie help? _____ Chrissy? _____ Cherie? _____

- How many customers did the 4 cashiers help all together? _____

- Would guessing an answer help you solve the problem? _____

- If your guess is wrong, can it still help you solve the problem? _____

- What problem-solving strategy can you use? _____

Solving problem 1: Decide with which cashier it would be better to start your guessing. Write your first guess on the back of this page. Then, based on that guess, figure out the number of customers helped by the other cashiers. Check your guess by finding a total and comparing it to 97. If your total is too high, make your next guess a lower number. If your total is too low, make your next guess a higher number.

Now use a similar procedure to solve two more problems.

Problem 2: To help the cashiers, the store manager decided to hire more baggers. On Monday, he posted a sign that read "Baggers wanted. Apply inside." On Tuesday, 2 more applications were received than on Monday. On Wednesday, 11 more than half the number of applications taken on Monday were received. If 53 applications were accepted during the first 3 days of the week, how many applications were received on Monday? _____

Problem 3: During her morning break, Chrissy snacked on muffins and read from her new paperback book. When her break was over, she used her bookmark to mark her stopping place. Between which 2 pages did Chrissy place the bookmark if the sum of the pages is 253? _____

Lessons for Teaching Problem-Solving Strategies

Lesson 5: Find a Pattern

Description of strategy: The find-a-pattern strategy is helpful when problem solvers have to analyze a numerical, visual, or behavioral pattern in data and then make a prediction or generalization based on that analysis. It may require problem solvers to extend a pattern or make a table to reveal a pattern.

Directions: Guide students to complete page 21 according to the instructions below.

Getting started: Have students read problem 1. Discuss the questions below one at a time, having students fill in the correct answers on their papers as you write them on the transparency.

- What are you to find out? *(the number of fans in line at 10:00 A.M. to buy tickets)*
- What time does the line start forming? *(8:45 A.M.)*
- How many fans start the line? *(4)*
- How many fans arrive 15 minutes later? *(8)*
- How does each new group of people joining the line increase compared to the previous group that lined up? *(the number doubles)*
- How can you use the rate of this increase to help you solve the problem? *(Record in a table the number of people joining the line every 15 minutes.)*
- Based on your answers, what problem-solving strategy could you use to solve the problem? *(find a pattern)*

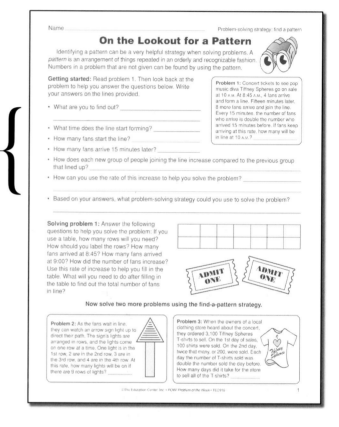

Solving problem 1: Guide students to set up a table to track the 15-minute time periods and the increasing number of fans joining the ticket line. Have students enter the times, the number of fans starting the line, and the number of fans joining the line 15 minutes later as shown. Next, have students complete the table by doubling each previous number entered. Then help students conclude that they should add to find the total number of fans in line *(252 fans).*

Time	8:45	9:00	9:15	9:30	9:45	10:00
Fans	4	8	16	32	64	128

Solving problems 2 and 3: Guide students through a similar procedure to solve the problems together as a class. Or have students solve the problems independently.

(2: 45 lights)

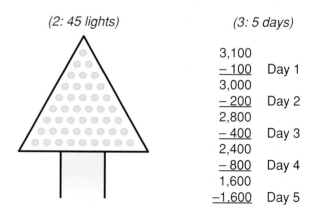

(3: 5 days)

3,100		
− 100	Day 1	
3,000		
− 200	Day 2	
2,800		
− 400	Day 3	
2,400		
− 800	Day 4	
1,600		
−1,600	Day 5	

On the Lookout for a Pattern

Identifying a pattern can be a very helpful strategy when solving problems. A *pattern* is an arrangement of things repeated in an orderly and recognizable fashion. Numbers in a problem that are not given can be found by using the pattern.

Getting started: Read problem 1. Then look back at the problem to help you answer the questions below. Write your answers on the lines provided.

Problem 1: Concert tickets to see pop music diva Tiffney Spheres go on sale at 10 A.M. At 8:45 A.M., 4 fans arrive and form a line. Fifteen minutes later, 8 more fans arrive and join the line. Every 15 minutes, the number of fans who arrive is double the number who arrived 15 minutes before. If fans keep arriving at this rate, how many will be in line at 10 A.M.? _____

• What are you to find out? _____

_____

• What time does the line start forming? _____

• How many fans start the line? _____

• How many fans arrive 15 minutes later? _____

• How does each new group of people joining the line increase compared to the previous group that lined up? _____

• How can you use the rate of this increase to help you solve the problem? _____

_____

• Based on your answers, what problem-solving strategy could you use to solve the problem?

_____

Solving problem 1: Answer the following questions to help you solve the problem: If you use a table, how many rows will you need? How should you label the rows? How many fans arrived at 8:45? How many fans arrived at 9:00? How did the number of fans increase? Use this rate of increase to help you fill in the table. What will you need to do after filling in the table to find out the total number of fans in line?

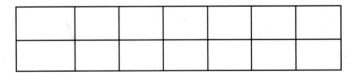

Now solve two more problems using the find-a-pattern strategy.

Problem 2: As the fans wait in line, they can watch an arrow sign light up to direct their path. The sign's lights are arranged in rows, and the lights come on one row at a time. One light is in the 1st row, 2 are in the 2nd row, 3 are in the 3rd row, and 4 are in the 4th row. At this rate, how many lights will be on if there are 9 rows of lights? _____

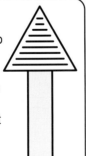

Problem 3: When the owners of a local clothing store heard about the concert, they ordered 3,100 Tiffney Spheres T-shirts to sell. On the 1st day of sales, 100 shirts were sold. On the 2nd day, twice that many, or 200, were sold. Each day the number of T-shirts sold was double the number sold the day before. How many days did it take for the store to sell all of the T-shirts? _____

Lessons for Teaching Problem-Solving Strategies

Lesson 6: Work Backward

Description of strategy: The work-backward strategy involves starting with the result or data given at the end of a problem and making a series of inverse computations to find the missing information.

Directions: Guide students to complete page 23 according to the instructions below.

Getting started: Have students read problem 1. Discuss the questions below one at a time, having students fill in the correct answers on their papers as you write them on the transparency.

- What are you to find out? *(the number of maps B. J. had on Monday)*
- What is B. J.'s job with the hiking club? *(keeping track of the club's hiking maps)*
- How many maps did the club president ask him to buy? *(12)*
- How many maps did B. J. loan to fellow hikers? *(6)*
- How many maps does B. J. have now? *(120)*
- Where did you find the information about the number of maps B. J. now has in the collection? *(at the end of the problem)*
- If you begin with the number of maps B. J. now has, what should you do to solve the problem? *(Work backward, using inverse operations to undo each previous step.)*

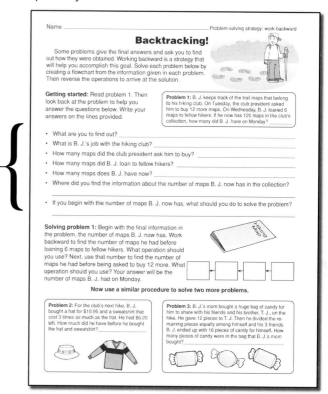

Solving problem 1: Guide students to begin with the final answer to the problem *(120 maps)* and work backward to find the number of maps B. J. had before loaning or buying any maps. Point out the last thing B. J. did *(loaned 6 maps)*. Explain that loaning compares to subtraction and that to work backward, students must use addition—the operation that reverses subtraction. Have students add 120 + 6 to get 126. Point out what B. J. did before loaning any maps *(bought 12 maps)*. Explain that buying compares to addition in this problem and that to work backward, students must use subtraction—the operation that reverses addition. Then have students subtract to get 114 *(126 – 12)*, the number of maps B. J. had on Monday.

| 114 | ← | – 12 | ← | + 6 | ← | 120 |

Solving problems 2 and 3: Guide students through a similar process to solve the problems together as a class. Or have students solve the problems independently. *(2: $49.00)*

| $49.00 | ← | + $10.95 | ← | + 3 ($10.95) | ← | $5.20 |

(3: 76 pieces)

| 76 | ← | + 12 | ← | x 4 | ← | 16 |

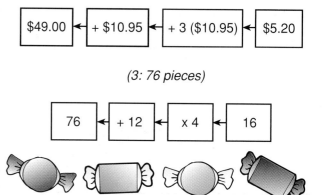

Backtracking!

Some problems give the final answers and ask you to find out how they were obtained. Working backward is a strategy that will help you accomplish this goal. Solve each problem below by creating a flowchart from the information given in each problem. Then reverse the operations to arrive at the solution.

Getting started: Read problem 1. Then look back at the problem to help you answer the questions below. Write your answers on the lines provided.

> **Problem 1:** B. J. keeps track of the trail maps that belong to his hiking club. On Tuesday, the club president asked him to buy 12 more maps. On Wednesday, B. J. loaned 6 maps to fellow hikers. If he now has 120 maps in the club's collection, how many did B. J. have on Monday? _____

- What are you to find out? _____
- What is B. J.'s job with the hiking club? _____
- How many maps did the club president ask him to buy? _____
- How many maps did B. J. loan to fellow hikers? _____
- How many maps does B. J. have now? _____
- Where did you find the information about the number of maps B. J. now has in the collection?

_____

- If you begin with the number of maps B. J. now has, what should you do to solve the problem?

_____

Solving problem 1: Begin with the final information in the problem, the number of maps B. J. now has. Work backward to find the number of maps he had before loaning 6 maps to fellow hikers. What operation should you use? Next, use that number to find the number of maps he had before being asked to buy 12 more. What operation should you use? Your answer will be the number of maps B. J. had on Monday.

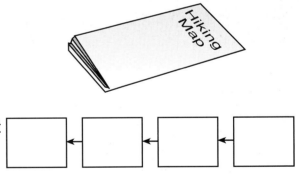

Now use a similar procedure to solve two more problems.

> **Problem 2:** For the club's next hike, B. J. bought a hat for $10.95 and a sweatshirt that cost 3 times as much as the hat. He had $5.20 left. How much did he have before he bought the hat and sweatshirt? _____

> **Problem 3:** B. J.'s mom bought a huge bag of candy for him to share with his friends and his brother, T. J., on the hike. He gave 12 pieces to T. J. Then he divided the remaining pieces equally among himself and his 3 friends. B. J. ended up with 16 pieces of candy for himself. How many pieces of candy were in the bag that B. J.'s mom bought? _____

Lessons for Teaching Problem-Solving Strategies

Lesson 7: Logical Reasoning

Description of strategy: The logical-reasoning strategy involves the use of conditional clues to help problem solvers arrive at a solution. Clues can be stated directly or implied. They can also be included in if-then statements. Displaying the data in a chart can help the problem solver work through the problem one statement at a time to arrive at the solution.

Directions: Guide students to complete page 25 according to the instructions below.

Getting started: Have students read problem 1. Discuss the questions below one at a time, having students fill in the correct answers on their papers as you write them on the transparency.

- What are you to find out? *(the color of each band member's shirt)*
- How many kids are in the band? *(4)*
- How many band members are boys? *(2)* Girls? *(2)*
- What is the shirt color of the boy standing next to Tina? *(blue)*
- What color is Tina's shirt? *(green)*
- What color is Laura's shirt? *(purple)*
- Would marking a logic box help you match the clues? *(yes)*
- What strategy could you use to solve the problem? *(logical reasoning)*

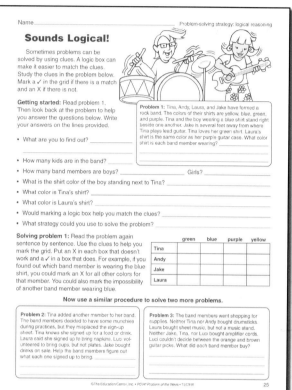

Solving problem 1: Guide students through the problem's clues. Since the boy next to Tina is wearing a blue shirt, mark the boxes in the blue column for Tina and Laura with an X. Since Jake is several feet away from Tina, he cannot be the boy wearing blue. Mark Jake's box in the blue column with an X. Since Andy's box is the only one without an X, he is wearing blue. Check Andy's box in the blue column. Then mark Xs in the other boxes in Andy's row. Mark that Tina is wearing green, but not blue, purple, or yellow; then mark the impossibility of other band members wearing green. Mark Laura's box to show she is wearing purple, but not another color; then mark the impossibility of other band members wearing purple. Finally, mark that Jake is wearing yellow since all the other colors are taken.
(Tina—green, Andy—blue, Jake—yellow, Laura—purple)

	green	blue	purple	yellow
Tina	✓	X	X	X
Andy	X	✓	X	X
Jake	X	X	X	✓
Laura	X	X	✓	X

Solving problems 2 and 3: Guide students through a similar process to solve the problems together as a class. Or have students solve the problems independently. *(2: Luci—cups, Tina—food, Laura—napkins, Andy—plates, Jake—drinks)*

	napkins	drinks	plates	food	cups
Luci	X	X	X	X	✓
Tina	X	X	X	✓	X
Laura	✓	X	X	X	X
Andy	X	X	✓	X	X
Jake	X	✓	X	X	X

(3: Jake—drumsticks, Tina—music stand, Andy—amplifier cords, Laura—sheet music, Luci—guitar picks)

	music stand	amplifier cords	drumsticks	sheet music	guitar picks
Jake	X	X	✓	X	X
Tina	✓	X	X	X	X
Andy	X	✓	X	X	X
Laura	X	X	X	✓	X
Luci	X	X	X	X	✓

Sounds Logical!

Sometimes problems can be solved by using clues. A logic box can make it easier to match the clues. Study the clues in the problem below. Mark a ✓ in the grid if there is a match and an X if there is not.

Getting started: Read problem 1. Then look back at the problem to help you answer the questions below. Write your answers on the lines provided.

Problem 1: Tina, Andy, Laura, and Jake have formed a rock band. The colors of their shirts are yellow, blue, green, and purple. Tina and the boy wearing a blue shirt stand right beside one another. Jake is several feet away from where Tina plays lead guitar. Tina loves her green shirt. Laura's shirt is the same color as her purple guitar case. What color shirt is each band member wearing? _____
_____
_____

• What are you to find out? _____
_____

• How many kids are in the band? _____

• How many band members are boys? _____ Girls? _____

• What is the shirt color of the boy standing next to Tina? _____

• What color is Tina's shirt? _____

• What color is Laura's shirt? _____

• Would marking a logic box help you match the clues? _____

• What strategy could you use to solve the problem? _____

Solving problem 1: Read the problem again sentence by sentence. Use the clues to help you mark the grid. Put an X in each box that doesn't work and a ✓ in a box that does. For example, if you found out which band member is wearing the blue shirt, you could mark an X for all other colors for that member. You could also mark the impossibility of another band member wearing blue.

	green	blue	purple	yellow
Tina				
Andy				
Jake				
Laura				

Now use a similar procedure to solve two more problems.

Problem 2: Tina added another member to her band. The band members decided to have some munchies during practices, but they misplaced the sign-up sheet. Tina knows she signed up for a food or drink. Laura said she signed up to bring napkins. Luci volunteered to bring cups, but not plates. Jake bought drinks on sale. Help the band members figure out what each one signed up to bring. _____
_____
_____

Problem 3: The band members went shopping for supplies. Neither Tina nor Andy bought drumsticks. Laura bought sheet music, but not a music stand. Neither Jake, Tina, nor Luci bought amplifier cords. Luci couldn't decide between the orange and brown guitar picks. What did each band member buy?
_____
_____
_____

Lessons for Teaching Problem-Solving Strategies

Lesson 8: Write an Equation

Description of strategy: Problem solvers use the write-an-equation strategy when they need to write a mathematical sentence to model information in a problem.

Directions: Guide students to complete page 27 according to the instructions below.

Getting started: Have students read problem 1. Discuss the questions below one at a time, having students fill in the correct answers on their papers as you write them on the transparency.

- What are you to do? *(represent the information in the problem)*
- Why is Louisiana Luke well known? *(He rescues frightened cats from treetops.)*
- What has he just done? *(tripled the number of cats he has rescued)*
- How many total cats has he brought safely to the ground? *(51)*
- If a number has tripled, what has it been multiplied by? *(3)*
- Do you know the number of cats rescued before it tripled? *(No, this information is unknown.)*
- How could you represent the number of cats he rescued before it tripled? *(Since that number is unknown, it could be represented with a variable.)*
- What strategy could you use to solve this problem? *(write an equation)*

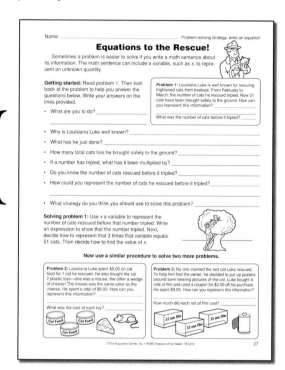

Solving problem 1: Guide students to use x to represent the number of cats before it tripled. Help them use the variable to write an expression showing that the number tripled *(3x).* Then help students write an equation to show that three times that variable equals 51 cats *(3x = 51).* Conclude by helping students understand that they should divide each side of the equation by 3 to find the value of x *(17).*

Solving problems 2 and 3: Guide students through a similar process to solve the problems together as a class. Or have students solve the problems independently.

(2: The toys cost $2.00 each.)
$$2x + \$5.00 = \$9.00$$
$$2x = \$9.00 - \$5.00$$
$$2x = \$4.00$$
$$x = \$2.00$$

(3: Each roll of film cost $3.00.)
$$4x - \$3.00 = \$9.00$$
$$4x = \$9.00 + \$3.00$$
$$4x = \$12.00$$
$$x = \$3.00$$

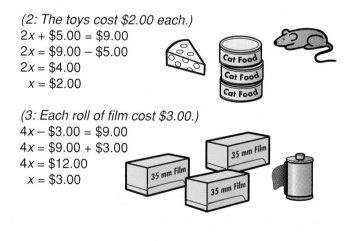

Name _____

Equations to the Rescue!

Sometimes a problem is easier to solve if you write a math sentence about its information. The math sentence can include a variable, such as *x,* to represent an unknown quantity.

Getting started: Read problem 1. Then look back at the problem to help you answer the questions below. Write your answers on the lines provided.

- What are you to do? _____
  _____

Problem 1: Louisiana Luke is well known for rescuing frightened cats from treetops. From February to March, the number of cats he rescued tripled. Now 51 cats have been brought safely to the ground. How can you represent this information? _____

_____

What was the number of cats before it tripled? _____

- Why is Louisiana Luke well known? _____

- What has he just done? _____

- How many total cats has he brought safely to the ground? _____

- If a number has tripled, what has it been multiplied by? _____

- Do you know the number of cats rescued before it tripled? _____

- How could you represent the number of cats he rescued before it tripled? _____
  _____

- What strategy do you think you should use to solve this problem? _____

Solving problem 1: Use *x* a variable to represent the number of cats rescued before that number tripled. Write an expression to show that the number tripled. Next, decide how to represent that 3 times that variable equals 51 cats. Then decide how to find the value of *x*.

Now use a similar procedure to solve two more problems.

Problem 2: Louisiana Luke spent $5.00 on cat food for 1 cat he rescued. He also bought the cat 2 plastic toys—one was a mouse, the other a wedge of cheese! The mouse was the same price as the cheese. He spent a total of $9.00. How can you represent this information? _____

_____

What was the cost of each toy? _____

Problem 3: No one claimed the last cat Luke rescued. To help him find the owner, he decided to put up posters around town bearing pictures of the cat. Luke bought 4 rolls of film and used a coupon for $3.00 off his purchase. He spent $9.00. How can you represent this information? _____

_____

How much did each roll of film cost? _____

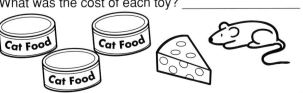

Lessons for Teaching Problem-Solving Strategies

Lesson 9: Choose the Correct Operation

Description of strategy: The choose-the-correct-operation strategy involves having problem solvers decide which mathematical operation to use: addition, subtraction, multiplication, or division. Sometimes more than one operation must be used. Identifying key words and phrases in a problem can suggest which operation is appropriate for solving a given problem.

Directions: Guide students to complete page 29 according to the instructions below.

Getting started: Have students read problem 1. Discuss the questions below one at a time, having students fill in the correct answers on their papers as you write them on the transparency.

- What are you to find out? (*the number of trays of water still available for the runners*)
- How many cups did Mrs. Fizzlewizzle fill? *(120)*
- How many cups of water were on each tray? *(15)*
- How many trays of water did she spill? *(3)*
- How can you find out the number of trays she had at the beginning? *(Divide the number of cups she filled [120] by the number of cups on each tray [15].)*
- How can you find out the number of trays she had after spilling 3 of them? *(Subtract 3 from the number of trays she had at the beginning.)*
- What strategy could you use? *(choose the correct operation)*

Solving problem 1: Guide students to look for words and phrases that suggest key concepts. Point out that finding the number of trays Mrs. Fizzlewizzle had in the beginning involves separating into groups *(dividing the number of cups filled by the number of cups on each tray)*. Help students conclude that they should divide 120 by 15 to get 8. Next, have students identify the concept that *spilling* suggests *(subtraction)*. Help students conclude that they should subtract 3 from 8 to get 5 *(the number of trays left)*. Finally, have students name the two operations used to solve the problem *(division and subtraction)*.

Solving problems 2 and 3: Guide students through a similar process to solve the problems together as a class. Or have students solve the problems independently. *(2: $1.65, addition and subtraction or subtraction and subtraction)*

$17.85 + $30.50 = $48.35
$50.00 − $48.35 = $1.65

(3: 237 decorations, multiplication and addition)

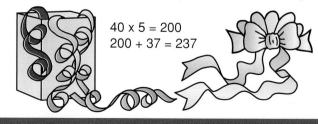

40 x 5 = 200
200 + 37 = 237

Make the Right Choice!

Before you can solve some problems, you must first decide whether to add, subtract, multiply, or divide. To help you decide, identify the problem's key concepts. You may have to use more than one operation to solve a problem.

Oh, dear! What should I do?

Subtract!
Divide!
Multiply!
Add!

Getting started: Read problem 1. Then look back at the problem to help you answer the questions below. Write your answers on the lines provided.

Problem 1: Mrs. Fizzlewizzle is in a frenzy. She is in charge of having cups of water available to runners during her city's annual marathon. She filled 120 cups with water and placed 15 cups on each tray. Then she accidentally spilled 3 trays of water. How many trays of water does she still have for the runners? _____ Which operation(s) did you use to solve the problem? _____

- What are you to find out? _____

- How many cups did Mrs. Fizzlewizzle fill? _____
- How many cups of water were on each tray? _____
- How many trays of water did she spill? _____
- How can you find out the number of trays she had at the beginning? _____
- How can you find out the number of trays she had after spilling 3 of them? _____
- What strategy could you use? _____

Solving problem 1: Reread the problem to look for words and phrases that suggest key concepts. If the concept is to put together, you should add. If the concept is to take away or compare, you should subtract. If the concept is to put equal sets together, you should multiply. If the concept is about separating into groups to find how many are in each group or how many groups, you should divide. (Hint: You will use 2 different operations to solve this problem.)

Now use a similar procedure to solve two more problems.

Problem 2: Mrs. Fizzlewizzle was also in charge of refreshments for the runners after the race. She had $50.00 to spend. She spent $17.85 for juice and $30.50 for apples and bananas. How much money did she have left? _____ Which operation(s) did you use to solve the problem?

_____

Problem 3: Mrs. Fizzlewizzle's husband was in charge of decorating both the starting line and finish line for the race. He filled 5 boxes each with 40 paper streamers. Then he made 37 colorful bows. How many decorations did he make? _____ Which operation(s) did you use to solve the problem?

_____

Lessons for Teaching Problem-Solving Strategies

Lesson 10: Solve a Simpler Problem

Description of strategy: The solve-a-simpler-problem strategy is used when a problem is too complex for problem solvers to solve in one step. A problem can be simplified by substituting smaller numbers for larger numbers or decreasing the number of given items. The simpler representation can then reveal a pattern or suggest what operation or process to use to solve the problem.

Directions: Guide students to complete page 31 according to the instructions below.

Getting started: Have students read problem 1. Discuss the questions below one at a time, having students fill in the correct answers on their papers as you write them on the transparency.

- What are you to find out? *(the number of tickets the station had at the beginning)*
- How many tickets did the station sell? *(¹/₂ of the total)*
- How many tickets did the station give away? *(¹/₄ of the remaining tickets)*
- Would the problem be easier to solve if you substituted a smaller number for 3,600? *(yes)*
- How could you make 3,600 smaller? *(36 x 100 = 3,600, so 36 could be the number of tickets given away.)*
- What strategy could you use? *(solve a simpler problem)*

Name _____   Problem-solving strategy: solve a simpler problem

Make It Simple!

Sometimes a complex problem is easier to solve if you substitute smaller numbers for larger numbers or decrease the number of given items. The simpler problem makes it easier to see a pattern or to know what operation or process to use to solve the problem.

Getting started: Read problem 1. Then look back at the problem to help you answer the questions below. Write your answers on the lines provided.

Problem 1: WMPS, a popular radio station, is sponsoring an outdoor concert to recognize the talent of two local bands that have cut their first CDs. It sold ½ of the tickets and gave away ¼ of the rest. If the station gave away 3,600 tickets, how many did it have in the beginning?

- What are you to find out? _____
- How many tickets did the station sell? _____
- How many tickets did the station give away? _____
- Would the problem be easier to solve if you substituted a smaller number for 3,600? _____
- How could you make 3,600 smaller? _____
- What strategy could you use? _____

Solving problem 1: Begin with 36, a simplified version of 3,600. Let it represent the number of tickets given away by the radio station. If 36 tickets = ¼ of the tickets given away, then figure out what ⁴/₄ would be. Let your answer represent ½ of the tickets. Then figure out what ²/₂ of that number would be. Finally, think back to how you used multiplication to simplify 3,600. Use what you learned to help you find the number of tickets the radio station had in the beginning.

Step 1: _____
Step 2: _____
Step 3: _____
Step 4: _____

Now use similar steps to solve two more problems.

Problem 2: Thanks to a local printing company, the radio station has pamphlets to promote the concert. Volunteers gave away ½ of the pamphlets at the mall and ⅓ of what was left at a weekend soccer tournament. If 550 pamphlets were given away at the soccer tournament, how many did the station have at first?

Problem 3: The radio station now has 300 of the bands' CDs. It gave away ¼ of the CDs it started with to listeners and ⅔ of the CDs it started with to concert volunteers. How many CDs did the station have to start with?

©The Education Center, Inc. • POW! Problem of the Week • TEC916   31

Solving problem 1: Guide students to think of 3,600 as 36 x 100. Then use 36 as the number of tickets given away by the radio station. If 36 tickets = ¹/₄ of the tickets given away, then ⁴/₄ (4 x 36) = 144 tickets before the giveaway. If 144 tickets = ¹/₂ of the tickets, then ²/₂ (2 x 144) = 288 tickets in the beginning. Then conclude that since 36 x 100 = 3,600 tickets given away, then 288 x 100 = 28,800 tickets at the beginning.

Step 1: 3,600 = 36 x 100
so 36 = tickets given away

Step 2: 36 = ¹/₄ of the unsold tickets
so ⁴/₄ (4 x 36) = 144, or half the tickets that were sold

Step 3: 144 = ¹/₂ of the tickets that were sold
so ²/₂ (2 x 144) = 288 tickets in the beginning

Step 4: 36 x 100 = 3,600
so 288 x 100 = 28,800 tickets

Solving problems 2 and 3: Guide students through similar steps to solve the problems together as a class. Or have students solve the problems independently. *(2: 3,300 pamphlets, 3: 1,200 CDs)*

Make It Simple!

This is WMPS, your We Make Problems Simpler station!

Sometimes a complex problem is easier to solve if you substitute smaller numbers for larger numbers or decrease the number of given items. The simpler problem makes it easier to see a pattern or to know what operation or process to use to solve the problem.

Getting started: Read problem 1. Then look back at the problem to help you answer the questions below. Write your answers on the lines provided.

> **Problem 1:** WMPS, a popular radio station, is sponsoring an outdoor concert to recognize the talent of two local bands that have cut their first CDs. It sold $\frac{1}{2}$ of the tickets and gave away $\frac{1}{4}$ of the rest. If the station gave away 3,600 tickets, how many did it have in the beginning?
>
> _____

- What are you to find out? _____
- How many tickets did the station sell? _____
- How many tickets did the station give away? _____
- Would the problem be easier to solve if you substituted a smaller number for 3,600? _____
- How could you make 3,600 smaller? _____
- What strategy could you use? _____

Solving problem 1: Begin with 36, a simplified version of 3,600. Let it represent the number of tickets given away by the radio station. If 36 tickets = $\frac{1}{4}$ of the tickets given away, then figure out what $\frac{4}{4}$ would be. Let your answer represent $\frac{1}{2}$ of the tickets. Then figure out what $\frac{2}{2}$ of that number would be. Finally, think back to how you used multiplication to simplify 3,600. Use what you learned to help you find the number of tickets the radio station had in the beginning.

Step 1: _____
_____

Step 2: _____
_____

Step 3: _____
_____

Step 4: _____
_____

Now use similar steps to solve two more problems.

> **Problem 2:** Thanks to a local printing company, the radio station has pamphlets to promote the concert. Volunteers gave away $\frac{1}{2}$ of the pamphlets at the mall and $\frac{1}{3}$ of what was left at a weekend soccer tournament. If 550 pamphlets were given away at the soccer tournament, how many did the station have at first?
>
> _____
>
>

> **Problem 3:** The radio station now has 300 of the bands' CDs. It gave away $\frac{1}{2}$ of the CDs it started with to listeners and $\frac{1}{4}$ of the CDs it started with to concert volunteers. How many CDs did the station have to start with? _____
>
>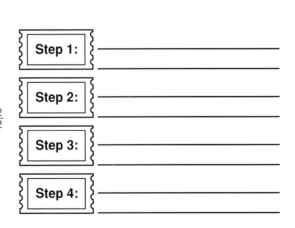

Louisiana Jones and the Buried Treasure

Finding a pattern

Teacher Page

Problem-solving strategies
students could use:
- work backward
- find a pattern
- guess and check
- act it out
- logical reasoning
- solve a simpler problem

Math skills
students will use:
- identify, extend, and use patterns
- draw conclusions
- use manipulatives
- test predictions

Restating the problem: Treasure hunters Louisiana Jones and Moe Money find an ancient treasure chest that is closed with ten silver bolts. To open the chest, Louisiana and Moe take turns pulling out one or two bolts at a time. The person who pulls out the last bolt wins the treasure. How can Louisiana try to make sure that she wins?

Important information found in the problem:
- The treasure chest has an inscription explaining how to open it.
- Only one person may win the treasure.
- There are ten bolts keeping the chest closed.
- Louisiana and Moe take turns pulling out one or two bolts at a time.
- No one may skip a turn.
- The person who pulls out the final bolt wins the treasure.

Answer Key Louisiana tried to make sure there were exactly 3 bolts left for Moe's last turn.

Bonus Box answer: The strategy remains the same.

Helpful Hints
Share this information when students get stuck to help put them back on the path to correctly solving the problem.

Hint 1 Practice the contest in pairs using ten small objects, such as counters or paper clips.

Hint 2 Take notes of each move in the practice contests. After playing five to ten rounds, look for a pattern in the winners' moves.

Hint 3 Work backward, starting with the final turn of removing either one or both bolts.

Hint 4 Try playing with fewer bolts. Make a generalization, comparing this smaller contest to the ten-bolt contest.

Louisiana Jones and the Buried Treasure

POW! #1

Round and round the world they roam,
Always traveling, never home,
Ne'er stopping to sleep or rest
Until they find the treasure chest
Buried in the days of old,
Crammed with jewels and coins of gold.

Have you heard the legend of treasure hunter Louisiana Jones and her sidekick, Moe Money? They challenged ancient curses (and modern security guards) in their search for hidden riches. But few people know what caused this raiding duo to finally go their separate ways. The split was over a treasure, as you might have suspected, but it was also over…a math problem.

One day in the dark jungles of South America, Louisiana and Moe unearthed an ancient metal trunk. According to their guidebook, *Treasure Hunting for Dummies,* the trunk contained millions of dollars' worth of jewels and gold coins. The chest was held shut by 10 silver bolts. On top of the chest was this inscription:

Two may find this chest,
but only one may have the treasure.
They must take turns removing the silver bolts,
pulling out either 1 or 2 per turn.
Whoever pulls out the final bolt keeps all the loot.
(And neither can skip a turn.)

Louisiana turned to Moe sadly. "Only one of us will win. I'm sorry to have to tell you this, but it's probably going to be me."

"Why you?" said Moe, his lower lip quivering.

"Because," said Louisiana Jones, "I paid attention in math class when we studied problem-solving strategies."

Now It's Your Turn
What strategy did Louisiana Jones use to try to make sure that she would win?

Bonus Box: What would happen if an odd number of bolts, such as 11, were used instead?

And Then There Was One

Using patterns to solve a problem

Problem-solving strategies

students could use:

- find a pattern
- make a list, table, or chart
- draw a picture or diagram
- act it out

Math skills

students will use:

- identify, extend, and use patterns
- make a table
- draw a diagram

Restating the problem: Mrs. Johnson gives her students a break from their regular math class by having a problem-solving contest. To win the contest, students must determine who the winner would be in a game. In the game, 25 students stand in a circle. The first person in the circle sits down. Every other student sits down until only one student is left standing. Which student is left standing?

Important information found in the problem:

- Twenty-five students stand in a circle.
- Student 1 sits down.
- Every other student sits down (Students 3, 5, 7, etc.).
- The pattern continues around the circle until only one student is left standing. That student is declared the winner of the game.

Answer Key Student 18 is the last one standing.

Bonus Box answer: Student 36

Helpful Hints

Share this information when students get stuck to help put them back on the path to correctly solving the problem.

Hint 1 Write the numbers 1 through 25 in a circle. Cross out every other number.

Hint 2 Try to solve a simpler version of the problem with fewer students.

Hint 3 Record your answer to the simpler problem in an input/output table. In the input column, write the number of students in the circle. In the output column, write the number of the winning student. Look for a pattern.

And Then There Was One

Spring seemed so far away, and everybody needed a break. It was too cold outside to use the playground at recess, the classroom smelled like old peanut butter, and winter vacation seemed like five years ago instead of five weeks ago. Luckily, Mrs. Johnson, the math teacher, had an idea.

"Today," she announced to her students, "we will not have math class."

The students cheered loud enough to wake up the class hamster. "Instead," Mrs. Johnson continued, "we will have a math contest that uses logic, reasoning, and advanced problem solving."

The cheers turned to moans and groans. The hamster went back to sleep. But Mrs. Johnson was not discouraged. "The winner," she added, "gets a homework pass for the rest of the week."

Now even the hamster was cheering! "To win the contest," explained Mrs. Johnson, "you must determine who the winner will be in a game. In the game, 25 students stand in a large circle. The teacher randomly chooses a student to be Student 1. That student is out of the game and must sit down. The next person clockwise in the circle, Student 2, remains standing. Student 3 sits down. This pattern continues around and around the circle until only one student is standing. Which student will that be?"

Now It's Your Turn
Figure out the number of the last student left standing.

Bonus Box: Which student would be the winner if there were 50 students in the circle?

Theater Seating

Finding the correct order in which five friends sit at the movies

Problem-solving strategies
students could use:
- logical reasoning
- make a list, table, or chart
- work backward
- guess and check
- draw a picture or diagram

Math skills
students will use:
- make generalizations
- draw conclusions
- make and test predictions
- use critical thinking
- make and interpret charts

Restating the problem: Five fans of old movies—Katharine, Shirley, Liz, Jimmy, and Bing—are very particular about where they sit when they go to the movie theater. In what order do the five friends sit?

Important information found in the problem:
- Five friends have a special order in which they sit at the movies.
- The tiny theater they attend has rows of five seats.
- Standing behind the seats facing the screen, Seat 1 is on the far left and Seat 5 is on the far right.
- Katharine insists on sitting at the end of the row.
- Shirley has to have someone on either side of her.
- Liz won't sit next to Shirley or Jimmy.
- Jimmy prefers sitting without anyone to his left.
- Bing will sit anywhere.

Answer Key As you face the movie screen, the friends are seated left to right as follows: Jimmy, Shirley, Bing, Liz, and Katharine.

Bonus Box answer: Jimmy was in *It's a Wonderful Life,* Shirley was in *The Little Princess,* Bing was in *High Society,* Liz was in *National Velvet,* and Katharine was in *Bringing Up Baby.*

Helpful Hints
Share this information when students get stuck to help put them back on the path to correctly solving the problem.

Hint 1 Make a seating chart numbered 1–5 from left to right.

Hint 2 Jot down names to show all the possible seats for each person. For example, Katharine could be in Seat 1 or 5 and Shirley could be in 2, 3, or 4.

Hint 3 Look for one person who can only sit in a particular seat, such as Jimmy, who must be in Seat 1 on the far left.

Hint 4 Each time one seat is claimed, look to see who has only one possible seat choice left and assign that seat to that person.

Hint 5 Experiment with several different arrangements. Then go slowly through the clues to find any problems.

Theater Seating

POW!
#3

They probably each had a normal, everyday kind of name, such as Julie, Josh, or Jenny.

But no one knew them by those names because they preferred to be called by their nicknames: Katharine, Shirley, Liz, Jimmy, and Bing.

The five friends were fans of old movies and their nicknames belonged to some pretty famous movie stars.

It's not easy to find a theater showing these movies anymore. But luckily there was one little theater down-town—so small that each row had only 5 seats—where they could watch vintage movies every Saturday afternoon.

High Society, It's a Wonderful Life, The Little Princess, National Velvet, and *Bringing Up Baby* were their favorites.

They were each pretty particular about where they sat. And they sat in the same seats every time they went to the theater.

Katharine insisted on sitting at the end of the row.

Shirley wanted to have someone on either side of her.

Liz wouldn't sit next to Shirley or Jimmy because they talked during the movies.

Jimmy was left-handed and preferred to sit without anyone to his left.

Bing wasn't picky; he'd sit anywhere.

Now It's Your Turn

Pretend you are standing behind a row of 5 seats, facing the screen. The first seat on the left is Seat 1 and the seat on the far right is Seat 5. Determine the order in which these 5 friends sit at the movies.

Bonus Box: Each friend is nicknamed for the star in her favorite movie. Use the clues below to figure out which star was in each movie.
- Katharine has a fondness for babies.
- Bing doesn't like plushy fabrics.
- Shirley loves anything to do with royalty.
- Jimmy loves life.

Kennel Quartet

Finding multiples and the least common multiple

Problem-solving strategies
students could use:
- make a list, table, or chart
- guess and check

Math skills
students will use:
- identify and extend patterns
- convert units of time
- list multiples
- find least common multiple
- calculate elapsed time

Restating the problem: Pop songwriter Joey Jingle works at a kennel to earn money. He wants to write a song featuring the barks and meows of the dogs and cats in the kennel. When will they meow and bark at the same time for the grand finale?

Important information found in the problem:
- Joey Jingle chooses two dogs to bark and two cats to meow in a song.
- Each animal makes noise at regular intervals.
- Arnie Airedale howls every four minutes.
- Polly Poodle yips every 30 seconds.
- Karen Kashmir meows softly every two minutes.
- Tony Tabby meows in a high pitch every five minutes.
- Joey gets all four animals to start at the same time. He must figure out when all four will bark and meow again at the same time.

Answer Key They will all bark and meow 20 minutes from the beginning of the song.

Bonus Box answer: They will flash together four times between midnight and 12:05 A.M.— 12:01:00 A.M., 12:02:00 A.M., 12:03:00 A.M., 12:04:00 A.M.

Helpful Hints
Share this information when students get stuck to help put them back on the path to correctly solving the problem.

Hint 1 Make a chart showing each animal's pattern, starting with when it begins barking or meowing. For example, Arnie Airedale's chart would show the following pattern: 4, 8, 12, and so on.

Hint 2 Look for the first common time that appears on all four charts.

Hint 3 The answer is the least common multiple of 4 minutes, 30 seconds or ½ minute, 2 minutes, and 5 minutes.

Kennel Quartet

POW! #4

Pop stars have it made! Most are rich and famous, and they get to travel all over the world. But what about the pop songwriters? They don't always have it so easy.

Take Joey Jingle, for example, a man who loves to write songs—classical, rock, rap, country, any kind of song. Unfortunately, no one was buying his music.

With money running short, he landed a job at the local animal shelter, where he watched over the dogs and cats from midnight to 6:00 A.M. All night long, he'd listen to the dogs bark and the cats meow.

Joey noticed that each dog had a different bark and each cat had a different meow. This gave him the idea of creating a song using animal noises.

He picked 4 animals with the best voices—Arnie Airedale, Polly Poodle, Karen Kashmir, and Tony Tabby. Then he timed their tones. He found that Arnie howled every 4 minutes, Polly yipped every 30 seconds, Karen meowed softly every 2 minutes, and Tony meowed in a high pitch every 5 minutes.

Joey Jingle thought he could get them all started at the same time. The problem was getting them to end the song with a grand finale: all four animals meowing and barking at the same time!

Now It's Your Turn

Help Joey figure out when all 4 animals will meow and bark at the same time.

Bonus Box: From the kennel, Joey could see the 24-hour diner where he liked to eat breakfast when he finished work. He noticed that the "Eat Here" neon sign flashed every 12 seconds and the "Good Food" sign flashed every 15 seconds. If both signs flashed at the same time at midnight, how many more times did they flash together again before 12:05 A.M.? List the times. (Include the hour, minute, and second in your answer.)

Heads Up!

Using clues to tell how many llamas and ostriches are in different fields

Problem-solving strategies
students could use:

- guess and check
- logical reasoning
- make a list, table, or chart
- draw a picture

Math skills
students will use:

- use multiples
- make an input-output table
- generate and continue number patterns

Restating the problem: Papa MacDonald and Mama MacDonald have farms with llamas and ostriches. Papa MacDonald counts heads and feet in his field, and Mama MacDonald counts eyes and feet in hers. Based on these clues, how many of each animal does Papa MacDonald own? Mama MacDonald?

Important information found in the problem:
- Papa MacDonald and Mama MacDonald have separate fields.
- Each of them has llamas and ostriches.
- Papa MacDonald counts 15 heads and 40 feet in his field.
- Mama MacDonald counts 30 eyes and 44 feet in her field.

Answer Key Papa MacDonald owns 5 llamas and 10 ostriches. Mama MacDonald owns 7 llamas and 8 ostriches.

Bonus Box answer: Answers will vary. Each problem should use 3 animals and 3 characteristics. Answers must be included.

Helpful Hints

Share this information when students get stuck to help put them back on the path to correctly solving the problem.

Hint 1 Using the number of heads as a clue, figure out how many animals Papa MacDonald has in all. Do the same for Mama MacDonald using the number of eyes.

Hint 2 Draw a sketch of a llama and an ostrich to count numbers of heads, eyes, and feet on each animal. *(Llamas have one head, two eyes, and four feet. Ostriches have one head, two eyes, and two feet.)*

Hint 3 Make a table showing the possible combinations of 15 animals for each farm. For example, if there are three ostriches on Papa's farm, there must be 12 llamas.

Hint 4 Include in the table the number of heads, eyes, and feet for each possibility. Notice the patterns in each column.

Heads Up!

Papa MacDonald had a farm. So did Mama MacDonald.

They used to work on the same farm, but she liked to do things her way and he liked to do things his way. So a few years back, they divided the farm between them.

"What kind of animals are you going to raise?" Mama MacDonald asked her husband.

"I'm not sure," he answered, "but I'm tired of hearing the usual barnyard sounds. All that cheep-cheep here, oink-oink there, here a moo, there a neigh, and everywhere a bowwow."

Mama MacDonald was tired of the usual sounds too. "E-I-E-I-O," she sang. "What does that mean anyway?"

So they decided to raise some new animals—llamas and ostriches! They planned to rent the llamas to hikers, who could use them to carry equipment. The ostriches' feathers would be sold as decorations.

They brought their animals home and divided them. Papa MacDonald put his animals in the north field and Mama MacDonald put hers in the south.

One day, Papa MacDonald exclaimed, "My animals are doing great! Why, just this morning I counted 15 heads and 40 feet in my field!"

Mama MacDonald replied, "Mine are doing well too. I counted 30 eyes and 44 feet in my field!"

Now It's Your Turn
Based on the clues about heads, eyes, and feet, figure out how many llamas and ostriches each of the MacDonalds has.

Bonus Box: Make up a similar problem using 3 types of animals and 3 characteristics. (Hint: Make sure to use animals that have at least 1 characteristic in common, such as 1 head, and at least 1 characteristic that's different, such as number of toes or type of body covering.) Don't forget to include the answer.

Lucky Leftovers

Dividing and then interpreting the remainder

Teacher Page

Problem-solving strategies
students could use:

- guess and check
- make a list, table, or chart
- draw a picture or diagram
- act it out
- solve a simpler problem

Math skills
students will use:

- write an equation
- interpret a remainder
- use the rules of divisibility

Restating the problem: A family reunion always ends with a friendly competition played in groups of three. Each group member holds up one or two fingers. The member holding up a different number of fingers advances. Anyone left out of a round because there aren't enough people to form a group of three automatically advances to the next round. How many rounds must be played to find a single winner?

Important information found in the problem:

- The game begins with 101 players.
- As many groups of three are formed as possible, with one or two players left over in every round but the final one.
- Each group has one member who advances to the next round. Anyone left over also advances to the next round.
- To play, each group member holds up either one or two fingers. The member holding up a different number of fingers advances to the next round. For example, if two group members each hold up two fingers, the third member holding up only one finger advances.
- If all three group members hold up the same number of fingers, the group plays again until there is one winner.
- The challenge is to figure out how many rounds must be played to find one winner.

Answer Key The Buffets must play five rounds to find a winner.

Bonus Box answer: The Stuffets also play five rounds to find a winner.

Helpful Hints

Share this information when students get stuck to help put them back on the path to correctly solving the problem.

Hint 1 Divide the number of people in each round by three. That's how many winners will go to the next round. Be sure to include the remainder (the number of people left over when groups of three are formed) in the next round.

Hint 2 Keep a chart or table showing how many people start each round, how many groups are made, and how many people are left over. Continue until there is one winner.

Hint 3 Act out the situation. Use a smaller number of people not divisible by three so students can understand what to do with the remainders.

Lucky Leftovers

The food at this year's Buffet family reunion was as delicious as ever. Folks feasted on barbecued chicken, baked beans, macaroni salad, hamburgers, hot dogs, cinnamon rolls, and toasted marshmallows.

But the reunion wasn't just about eating. There was swimming, fishing, hide-and-seek, tag, card games, and campfire songs. By Sunday afternoon, the reunion was coming to an end. But before everyone loaded up the cars and headed home, there was the much anticipated, traditional competition to see who'd get to take home all of the delicious leftover food!

All 101 Buffets gathered to play a game so simple even the youngest cousins could play! Here's what they did.

1. They all divided into groups of 3.
2. Each group member held up 1 or 2 fingers.
3. The group member who advanced was the one who held up a different number of fingers from the other 2 in the group. For example, if 2 group members held up 2 fingers, the third member holding up 1 finger advanced. (If all 3 group members held up the same number of fingers, the group played again until there was a winner.)

In the first round, the 101 Buffets made 33 groups of 3, with 2 people left over. Each group had 1 winner who moved on to the second round. The 2 people left over also moved on to the second round. The game continued until there was just 1 winner—the luckiest Buffet of all!

Now It's Your Turn
How many rounds did the Buffets play in order to eliminate everyone but the final winner?

Bonus Box: The Stuffets next door liked the way the Buffets determined who got the leftovers, and they decided to copy it. The Stuffets have 157 people in their family. How many rounds did they play to eliminate all but the final winner?

Worth the Change?

Finding the number and type of coins pulled from a pie

Problem-solving strategies
students could use:

- guess and check
- make a list, table, or chart
- write an equation
- choose the correct operation

Math skills
students will use:

- use multiples
- relate money to decimals
- look for a pattern
- use coin value relationships
- add and multiply decimals
- write and evaluate algebraic expressions

Restating the problem: Little Jack Horner pulls twice as many nickels as quarters and three times as many dimes as quarters from a pie. If there are 24 coins, how many of each type of coin does he have? What is the total value?

Important information found in the problem:
- Jack pulls a combination of quarters, dimes, and nickels out of a pie.
- There are 24 coins in all.
- There are twice as many nickels as quarters.
- There are three times as many dimes as quarters.

Answer Key There are four quarters, eight nickels, and 12 dimes. The total is $2.60.

Bonus Box answer: One solution: six quarters, 12 dimes, 18 nickels, and three pennies. The total is $3.63. Another solution: five quarters, ten dimes, 15 nickels, and nine pennies. The total is $3.09.

Helpful Hints

Share this information when students get stuck to help put them back on the path to correctly solving the problem.

Hint 1 Use manipulatives to model the problem. Try dividing 24 counters into three groups in a way that fits the clues. Make Group 2 twice as large as Group 1 and Group 3 three times as large as Group 1.

Hint 2 Write an equation. For example, let x = the number of quarters. If there are twice as many nickels as quarters, then $2x$ = the number of nickels. If there are three times as many dimes as quarters, then $3x$ = the number of dimes. Write the terms as an equation: $x + 2x + 3x = 24$. Simplify to $6x = 24$, with $x = 4$. Then find the number of nickels and dimes.

Hint 3 Once the number of each type of coin is known, calculate the total value. Multiply the number of each type of coin by its value: 4 quarters x $0.25, 8 nickels x $0.05, and 12 dimes x $0.10. Add to get the total value.

Worth the Change?

Should nursery rhymes be changed?

Just imagine it! Little Miss Muffet eating pizza instead of curds and whey. Humpty Dumpty wearing cushioned body armor. And the old woman who lived in a shoe moving to the city.

Maybe the changes are okay, but what about all the kids who've been repeating the rhymes for years and years? What would they say if Little Jack Horner pulled coins from his pie instead of a plum? Just listen to this:

Little Jack Horner
Sat in a corner,
Eating his blueberry pie;
He plunged in his hand,
And found coins—how grand!
And said, "What a rich boy am I!"

Is there enough money in the pie to make it worth changing the rhyme? Let's see! Suppose Jack pulls 24 coins out of the pie: a combination of nickels, dimes, and quarters. Say he counts twice as many nickels as quarters and 3 times as many dimes as quarters. How many coins of each type does he have? What is the total value of the 24 coins?

Now It's Your Turn
Find out how many of the 24 coins are nickels, dimes, and quarters. Also determine the total value of the coins. Remember, there are twice as many nickels as quarters and 3 times as many dimes as quarters.

Bonus Box: Jack reached into a second pie and found 39 coins! This time there are 3 times as many nickels as quarters, twice as many dimes as quarters, and fewer than 10 pennies. How many of each type of coin is in the pie? What is the total value of the 39 coins? (Hint: There are 2 possible answers.)

Nickel Mania

Comparing the value of a mile-high stack of nickels to a million nickels

POW! #8

Problem-solving strategies
students could use:
- make a list, table, or chart
- choose the correct operation

Math skills
students will use:
- establish coin-value relationships
- measure with tools, such as a ruler, yardstick, or measuring tape
- multiply and subtract decimals
- convert customary units
- compare and order decimals

Restating the problem: A billionaire offers college scholarships to students who can solve a problem. Which is worth more: a million nickels or a mile-high stack of nickels? How much more?

Important information found in the problem:
- The Downtown University of Middling isn't attracting many students.
- To attract students, billionaire Homer Nickels offers scholarships to students who can solve a problem.
- To earn a scholarship, students must determine which is worth more: a million nickels or a mile-high stack of nickels.

Answer Key One million nickels equals $50,000.00. There are 13 nickels in one inch, so a mile-high stack would be worth $41,184.00. Therefore, one million nickels is worth $8,816.00 more than a mile-high stack.

Bonus Box answer: Answers will vary. Students multiply their height in inches by $0.17. For example, a four-foot stack would be worth $8.16, a 4½-foot stack would be worth $9.18, and a five-foot stack would be worth $10.20.

Helpful Hints
Share this information when students get stuck to help put them back on the path to correctly solving the problem.

Hint 1 Make a one-inch high stack of nickels and count them. *(1 inch = 13 nickels)*

Hint 2 There are 12 inches in a foot and 5,280 feet in a mile, so there are 63,360 inches in a mile.

Hint 3 Find the number of nickels in a mile by multiplying the number of inches in one mile times the number of nickels in one inch *(63,360 x 13 = 823,680 nickels)*.

OR

Find the number of nickels in a foot by multiplying the number of inches in one foot by the number of nickels in one inch *(12 x 13 = 156 nickels)*. Then find the number of nickels in a mile by multiplying the number of feet in one mile by the number of nickels in one foot *(5,280 x 156 = 823,680 nickels)*.

Hint 4 Find the value of a mile-high stack of nickels by multiplying the number of nickels in the stack by $0.05 *(823,680 x $0.05 = $41,184.00)*.

Hint 5 Find the value of a million nickels by multiplying one million by $0.05 *(1,000,000 x $0.05 = $50,000.00)*.

Hint 6 Compare the two values to find which is greater *($50,000.00 > $41,184.00)*. Then subtract to find the difference *($50,000.00 – $41,184.00 = $8,816.00)*.

Nickel Mania

POW!
#8

Billionaire Homer Nickels was quite proud of his hometown of Middling. It had beautiful parks, wonderful public schools, prosperous businesses, and friendly people.

But for some reason, the Downtown University of Middling (popularly known as D. U. M.) wasn't attracting many students.

That made Homer Nickels very sad indeed. So he went to the president of D. U. M. and made the following offer:

"I will donate millions and millions of dollars to your university on two conditions. First, you must change the name. It's obvious that students do not want to go to a school named D. U. M. We could call the school Nickels University for Technology Students!"

The president didn't think that offer would improve the situation much, but she patiently waited to hear the second condition.

"Secondly," Homer Nickels explained, "we need a publicity stunt to get our name noticed. I will offer a scholarship to anyone who can tell me which is worth more: a million nickels or a mile-high stack of nickels. What do you think of my idea?"

"I think it's nuts," replied the president. "But I guess it's worth a try!"

Now It's Your Turn
Figure out which is worth more: a million nickels or a mile-high stack of nickels. Then find the difference between the two amounts.

Bonus Box: Suppose there were 17 pennies to an inch. If you made a stack of pennies equal to your height, what would it be worth? Show your calculations.

Flag Talk

Changing fractions to percents

Problem-solving strategies
students could use:

- draw a picture or diagram
- write an equation

Math skills
students will use:

- change fractions to percents
- add fractions
- identify equivalent fractions
- write fractions in simplest terms
- round decimals to the nearest hundredth

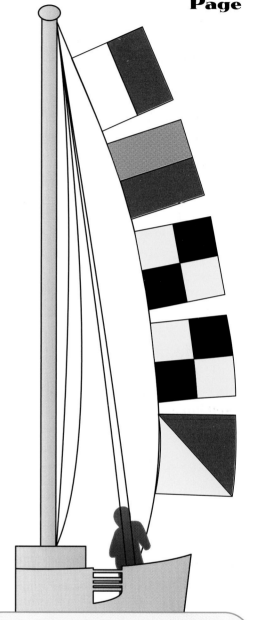

Restating the problem: Skipper's teacher has caught him writing a note in flag code during math class. Now Skipper must find the percentages of certain colors on each flag. What percentage does each boldfaced color represent? What does Skipper's message say?

Important information found in the problem:
- The international flag code is used to send messages at sea. Each letter of the alphabet is represented by a different flag.
- The flag code uses five colors: red, white, blue, yellow, and black.
- Skipper wrote a message using the flag code.
- Skipper's teacher asked him to find the percentages of certain colors used in his message's flags.

Answer Key

Flag 1—¹/₅, 0.20, 20% (red)
Flag 2—¹/₂, 0.50, 50% (blue)
Flag 3—¹/₂, 0.50, 50% (blue)
Flag 4— ¹/₂, 0.50, 50% (white)
Flag 5—¹/₂, 0.50, 50% (yellow)
Flag 6—¹/₂, 0.50, 50% (black)
Flag 7—¹/₂, 0.50, 50% (blue)

Flag 8—¹/₂, 0.50, 50% (red)
Flag 9—⁵/₉, 0.56, 56% (yellow)
Flag 10—¹/₃, 0.33, 33% (red)
Flag 11—¹/₂, 0.50, 50% (white)

Luke,
    Go to the rock. Get net.

Bonus Box answer:
Flags 2, 3, 5, and 7 are 50% blue.
Flags 3, 5, 6, and 8 are 50% yellow.
Flags 4, 7, and 11 are 50% white.
Flags 2, 4, 8, and 11 are 50% red.

Helpful Hints
Share this information when students get stuck to help put them back on the path to correctly solving the problem.

Hint 1 Write a fraction to represent each flag's underlined color. Then change each fraction to a decimal and each decimal to a percent.

Hint 2 Change each fraction to a decimal by dividing the numerator by the denominator. Round the decimal quotient to the nearest hundredth if necessary.

Flag Talk

POW! #9

The ship rocked from side to side as the waves crested higher and higher before crashing down on the deck. "We're going down, Skipper!" yelled Luke, the first mate. "Only a miracle can save us!"

"Never fear," answered Skipper, gripping the ship's wheel to steer through the perilous breakers. "Raise the flags to send a message!"

"Skipper, are you with us?" asked Mr. Jennings, his math teacher.

"Ah…sure, Mr. Jennings," replied Skipper, awakening from his daydream. "Percentages, right?"

That's Skipper for you. Always thinking and reading about sailing the seas. Recently, Skipper read about the international flag code, which uses flags of different designs to represent each letter of the alphabet. "This will be useful," he thought. "I can practice my nautical skills by writing in flag code during class."

Today, as he was writing a note in flag code, his math teacher caught him. "What's this?" Mr. Jennings questioned sternly.

"Uh…it's math in flag code," replied Skipper.

"Well, then," the teacher said, "prove you understand the lesson I just taught. Find the percentage of each color I indicate on your flags. I'll be back to check your work."

1

| blue |
| white |
| **red** |
| white |
| blue |

C

2

| **blue** |
| red |

E

3

| yellow | blue | yellow | blue | yellow | blue |

G

4

| **white** | red |

H

5

| **yellow** | blue |

K

6

| yellow | **black** |
| **black** | yellow |

L

7

blue	white	**blue**	white
white	**blue**	white	**blue**
blue	white	**blue**	white
white	**blue**	white	**blue**

N

8

| | **red** |
| yellow | |

O

9

red	**yellow**	red
yellow	yellow	yellow
red	yellow	red

R

10

| **red** | white | blue |

T

11

| red | **white** |
| **white** | red |

U

Now It's Your Turn

The flags Skipper used in his note are shown above. Color each flag according to the labels. Find the percentage of each flag's boldfaced color. Then use the flags to decode Skipper's message.

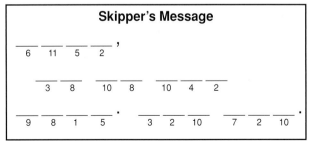

Skipper's Message

___ ___ ___ ___ ,
6   11   5   2

___ ___ ___ ___ ___ ___ ___
3   8   10   8   10   4   2

___ ___ ___ ___ . ___ ___ ___ ___ ___ ___ .
9   8   1   5   3   2   10   7   2   10

Bonus Box: Which flags are 50% blue? 50% yellow? 50% white? 50% red?

Note to the teacher: Students will need crayons or markers in the following colors to complete this page: red, blue, yellow, and black.

Getting a Fair Share

Making equivalent fractions

Problem-solving strategies
students could use:

• guess and check
• make a list, table, or chart
• write an equation

Math skills
students will use:

• simplify fractions
• use fractions equal to or greater than one
• find equivalent fractions
• compare fractions

Restating the problem: Twins Jack and Jill, who insist on dividing everything equally, challenge their classmates to solve an equivalency problem. Using the incomplete equation $^6/\_ = \_/_4$ and the digits 1 to 9, how many pairs of equivalent fractions can their classmates make?

Important information found in the problem:
• Twins Jack and Jill like to divide everything equally, but not exactly the same. Because of this, they learn a lot about equivalent fractions.
• The twins challenge their classmates to find as many pairs of equivalent fractions for a given equation as possible. One fraction has a numerator of six and the other a denominator of four.
• Any number from one to nine can be used to complete the fractions.

Answer Key There are the following four pairs of equivalent fractions:

$$^6/_6 = {}^4/_4 \qquad ^6/_4 = {}^6/_4$$
$$^6/_3 = {}^8/_4 \qquad ^6/_8 = {}^3/_4$$

Bonus Box answer: The following four equivalent fractions are formed:

$$^6/_1 = {}^{24}/_4 \qquad ^6/_{12} = {}^2/_4$$
$$^6/_2 = {}^{12}/_4 \qquad ^6/_{24} = {}^1/_4$$

Helpful Hints

Share this information when students get stuck to help put them back on the path to correctly solving the problem.

Hint 1 Solve the problem methodically. Use each number from one through nine in the first fraction. Then try different number choices to make the second fraction equivalent to the first.

Hint 2 Reducing the new fractions to their simplest form may help students spot equivalencies.

Hint 3 Think creatively. Can identical fractions be formed? What about improper fractions, or fractions equal to one?

Getting a Fair Share

Fair is fair! That was the motto of the twins.

Jack and Jill always insisted that everything be divided equally between them.

"Fifty-fifty!" exclaimed Jack.

"Half and half!" agreed Jill.

But actually, they really didn't want to be *exactly* the same. So from a very early age, they thought of different ways to express the same thing. That way, they could be…

"Separate but equal!" exclaimed Jill.

"Two different peas in a pod!" agreed Jack.

They were very excited the day they discovered that the same number could be expressed in different ways. For example, Jack received $3.00 for allowance, while Jill collected 12 quarters. One year on their birthday, Jill celebrated turning ten, while Jack rejoiced over turning 120 months!

One day in math class, the lesson was about equivalent fractions. As you can imagine, this was not a hard topic for the twins, who'd been practicing equivalencies for years. So they challenged the rest of the class to solve a problem they made up.

"Suppose I start a fraction by writing a 6 as the numerator and another fraction by writing a 4 as the denominator," began Jill.

"Using only the digits 1 to 9, fill in the missing numbers to make as many pairs of equivalent fractions as possible," added Jack.

Jill wrote the problem on the board. "That will be your homework class," she announced. "*Our* homework will be to make an answer key!"

Now It's Your Turn
How many different ways can you make the two fractions equal by filling in the missing numerator and denominator with the numbers 1–9?

Bonus Box: If you solved the same problem using any numbers from 1 to 25, how many more equivalent fractions could you make? List them.

Alien Mathematics

Decoding symbols used to represent the numbers 0–9

Problem-solving strategies

students could use:
- guess and check
- make a list, table, or chart
- logical reasoning
- find a pattern

Math skills

students will use:
- make and test predictions
- evaluate algebraic expressions
- solve for variables
- estimate sums
- understand place value

Restating the problem: An alien planet receives a cryptic communication containing symbols written as an addition problem. Which number from 0–9 does each symbol represent?

Important information found in the problem:
- Aliens on Planet Zythgrp receive a message containing symbols written as an addition problem.
- Each symbol represents a number from 0 to 9.
- A symbol always represents the same number.
- No number is represented by more than one symbol.
- The top line plus the middle line equals the bottom line.
- Each column of numbers has to be regrouped.

Answer Key ⚛ = 1, ◉ = 9, 🛸 = 0, ⚕ = 2, ☼ = 8

Bonus Box answer: Students' problems will vary, but the value of each symbol should match those listed in the answer key above.

Helpful Hints

Share this information when students get stuck to help put them back on the path to correctly solving the problem.

Hint 1 Copy the problem. To the right of each symbol, pencil in one digit at a time to try different number combinations. Continue guessing, checking, and revising until the solution has been found.

Hint 2 Use logic to figure out certain values. For example, ⚛ must equal 1 because the problem's answer has a number in the thousands column. Therefore, a 1 has to be regrouped to that column. The ◉ symbol must equal 9 because that column needs a number which equals 10 or more when added to 1, making regrouping necessary.

Hint 3 After plugging in all of the 1s, it's clear that 🛸 must equal 0 because 9 + 1 = 10.

Hint 4 Once the values of ⚛, ◉, and 🛸 are known, guess and check to find the values of ☼ and ⚕.

Alien Mathematics

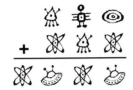

POW! #11

What language would be used if humans and aliens ever made contact? It probably wouldn't be English or Spanish or Mandarin!

One theory is that math would be the language that links people and aliens, perhaps because the laws of math are thought to be true no matter what planet you're on.

Recently on Planet Zythgrp, 3 Zythgrpians watched the following mysterious message blip onto a computer monitor at their workstation.

"What is *this?*" asked Trowbnz. "It sure doesn't look like the zizzarball scores from the Intergalactic League."

"That's for sure! Maybe it's a communication from that blue-green planet over there," suggested Klmev, pointing out the window.

Trowbnz gasped in horror. "Could this mean there is intelligent life on Earth?" Then Klmev and Trowbnz chuckled and went back to surfing the Galaxy Wide Web.

But the third Zythgrpian, Ygdfr, began to study the symbols. He quickly came to the following conclusions:

- Each symbol represents a number from 0 to 9.
- A symbol always represents the same number.
- No number is represented by more than 1 symbol.
- The top line plus the middle line equals the bottom line.
- Each column of numbers has to be regrouped.

That was all he needed to know to figure out which number each symbol represented.

"If there's not intelligent life on Earth," he announced to his friends, "then the boss's kids are here goofing around on the computers again."

Now It's Your Turn

Figure out which number from 0–9 each symbol represents in the addition problem.

Bonus Box: Use the symbols in the problem above to create a similar addition problem for a classmate to solve.

Cross-Country Miles

Calculating the distance driven the first and last days on a cross-country trip

Problem-solving strategies

students could use:

- work backward
- guess and check
- make a list, table, or chart
- draw a picture or diagram
- write an equation

Math skills

students will use:

- make and test predictions
- use variables
- write and solve algebraic equations
- divide whole numbers
- round to the nearest whole number

Restating the problem: A family spends five days driving about 2,800 miles across the United States from Washington, DC, to San Francisco, California. Each day they drive 100 miles less than on the previous day. How many miles do they drive on the first day? The last day?

Important information found in the problem:

- The trip from Washington, DC, to San Francisco, California, is about 2,800 miles.
- The trip takes five days.
- The family drives the farthest on the first day.
- Each day after that, they drive 100 miles less than they did the day before.

Answer Key They drove 760 miles on the first day and 360 miles on the last day.

Bonus Box answer: They drove about 13 hours on the first day and about 6 hours on the last day.

Helpful Hints

Share this information when students get stuck to help put them back on the path to correctly solving the problem.

Hint 1 Find the average daily mileage if the family had traveled equal distances each day. Divide the total distance (2,800 miles) by the number of days (five). This represents the middle day of the trip. Then work backward to the first day and forward to the last day.

Hint 2 Use a variable to write an equation representing the mileage driven each day during the 2,800-mile trip. Let x represent the mileage driven on Day 1, $x - 100$ represent the mileage for Day 2, $x - 200$ the mileage for Day 3, and so on. Solve the resulting equation—$x + (x - 100) + (x - 200) + (x - 300) + (x - 400) = 2,800$ miles—to find the value of x (760). Then subtract 400 from the value of x to find the final day's mileage (360).

Cross-Country Miles

Ask Mikey Miles how long it takes to drive from Washington, DC, to San Francisco, California. He should know. He just spent 5 days in the back of his family's car with Meggie and Maggy, his older sisters!

"How long does it take?" asked Mikey. "Long enough to read 29 comic books, play 93 card games, eat 13 peanut butter and jelly sandwiches, and spill a dozen drinks. It's a cool trip, seeing all the mountains and farms and rivers and canyons, but it sure is a long one."

Mikey's parents knew their kids would need longer breaks as their 2,800-mile journey continued.

On the first day, when no one was the least bit tired, they drove the farthest, stopping only to eat or fill the car with gas.

On the second day, the family wasn't feeling quite as fresh and excited, so they drove 100 miles less than they did on the first day. This gave them time for a long picnic.

On the third day, the family was getting tired of being in the car, so they drove 100 miles less than they did on the second day. This gave them time to go swimming for a couple of hours.

And so they continued, each day driving 100 miles less than they did the day before, until they arrived in San Francisco at the end of the fifth day.

What did Mikey Miles say when they arrived? "Not a moment too soon! Could we *please* fly home?"

Now It's Your Turn
How many miles did Mikey's family drive on the first day of their 2,800-mile trip? The last day?

Bonus Box: If Mikey's parents averaged 60 miles per hour during their drive, about how many hours did they drive on the first day? The last day? (Hint: Round your answers to the nearest whole number.)

Sports Quandary

Problem-solving strategies
students could use:

- guess and check
- make a list, table, or chart

Math skills
students will use:

- compare and order whole numbers
- use a Venn diagram
- estimate and compute sums and differences

Restating the problem: Zachary has his coach use a set of clues to figure out how many students will play each sport. How many students will be on each team? How many will play only volleyball and basketball? How many will play only volleyball and soccer?

Important information found in the problem:

- Three sports—volleyball, basketball, and soccer—are offered to 86 students.
- Each student must sign up for at least one sport but can also sign up to play two sports or all three.
- The same number of students signed up for each of the three sports.
- Seventy-five students signed up for one sport, nine for two sports, and two for three sports.
- No one signing up for two sports chose both basketball and soccer.
- Twenty-five students want to play only basketball. That is three more than the number who want to play only volleyball and three less than the number who want to play only soccer.

Answer Key Each team will have 33 students. Six students will play only volleyball and basketball. Three students will play only volleyball and soccer.

Bonus Box answer: Five more students played soccer than volleyball. Five more students played volleyball than basketball.

Helpful Hints

Share this information when students get stuck to help put them back on the path to correctly solving the problem.

Hint 1 Some students may need to read aloud and discuss the meaning of each clue.

Hint 2 Draw a Venn diagram with three overlapping circles, each labeled with a different sport: volleyball, basketball, and soccer. Write 2 in the section where all three circles overlap. This represents the two students who are going to play all three sports. Write 0 in the area where basketball and soccer overlap. This represents that no students want to play a combination of basketball and soccer. Next, write 25 in the part of the basketball circle that does not overlap with any other circle. This represents the students who will play only basketball. Using similar clues, write 22 in the volleyball-only portion and 28 in the soccer-only portion.

Hint 3 Add 2 + 0 + 25 + 22 + 28 to get 77 of the 86 total students. Divide the remaining nine students between the two unlabeled sections where volleyball overlaps basketball and volleyball overlaps soccer.

Hint 4 Use guess and check to determine the placement of the remaining nine students, keeping in mind that all three sports must have the same total number of players.

Hint 5 Add all of the numbers within each sport's circle to determine the number of students playing that sport.

Sports Quandary

Coach Carr announced that this year all 86 of his students would play on at least one team: volleyball, basketball, or soccer. If a student wanted to play on more than one team, that would be okay too!

The coach passed around the sign-up sheets for each sport. The last student to get them was Zachary Mack, an excellent thinker who would rather work on his computer than play a sport. He reluctantly signed up for a sport and then looked over the three lists.

"Well, Zach," said the coach, "how many signed up for each sport?"

"Coach," Zach countered, "suppose I give you a few clues about the lists. If you can use the clues to figure out how many students will play each sport, then I'll go out for all 3 teams. But if you can't, then I won't have to play at all."

The coach waited while Zach read aloud these clues:
- The same number of students signed up for each of the 3 sports.
- Seventy-five signed up to play only 1 sport, 9 to play only 2 sports, and 2 to play all 3 sports.
- No one who signed up for 2 sports chose both basketball and soccer.
- Twenty-five students want to play only basketball. This is 3 more than the number who want to play only volleyball and 3 less than the number who want to play only soccer.

The coach blew his whistle. "Here's the answer, Zach. See you for volleyball, basketball, and soccer!"

Now It's Your Turn

Based on Zach's clues, how many students will be on each team? How many will play only volleyball and basketball? How many will play only volleyball and soccer?

Bonus Box: Last year, Coach Carr had 5 students who played all 3 sports. These 5 students made up 25% of the volleyball team, $\frac{1}{3}$ of the basketball team, and 20% of the soccer team. How many more students played soccer than volleyball? How many more played volleyball than basketball?

Mystery Boxes

Using clues to figure out the weights of four boxes

Teacher Page

Problem-solving strategies
students could use:
- guess and check
- make a list, table, or chart
- find a pattern

Math skills
students will use:
- estimate sums
- use basic operations
- use powers and exponents
- find common multiples
- find factors of a number

Restating the problem: Four sealed boxes sit in a classroom. The teacher gives her students four clues to help them determine the weight of each box. How much does each box weigh?

Important information found in the problem:
- Students want to know what's in four sealed boxes.
- The teacher gives this information about the weight of the four boxes:
    The weight of Box 1 squared equals the weight of Box 2.
    The weight of Box 2 squared equals the weight of Box 4.
    Box 3's weight is a multiple of Boxes 1 and 2 and a factor of Box 4.
- The total weight of all four boxes is 120 pounds.

Answer Key Box 1—3 lb., Box 2—9 lb., Box 3—27 lb., Box 4—81 lb. The pattern may be expressed two ways: (1) each box is three times the weight of the previous box or (2) the weight of each successive box is 3 to the next higher power: $3^1 = 3$, $3^2 = 9$, $3^3 = 27$, and $3^4 = 81$.

Bonus Box answer: The total weight would be 340 lb. (4 + 16 + 64 + 256).

Helpful Hints
Share this information when students get stuck to help put them back on the path to correctly solving the problem.

Hint 1 Start with a guess-and-check approach. Pick any number to be the weight of Box 1. Use that number to calculate the weights of Boxes 2 and 4. (Square the weight of Box 1 to get the weight of Box 2. Square the weight of Box 2 to get the weight of Box 4.)

Hint 2 If the sum of those three numbers is greater than 120, try a smaller guess for Box 1.

Hint 3 If the sum of those three numbers is less than 120, figure out what the weight of Box 3 must be to make the sum equal 120. Then test that guess to make sure the number is a multiple of Boxes 1 and 2 and a factor of Box 4.

Hint 4 Use a table to record the outcome of each guess.

Hint 5 To find the pattern, write the numbers 3, 9, 27, and 81 as a series. Then determine the rule that governs the series.

Mystery Boxes

Mrs. Dibble has always asked lots of questions.

Some of the questions are the kind you'd expect from a teacher, such as "Which planet is nearest to the sun?" and "Where is your homework?"

But not all of Mrs. Dibble's questions are so straightforward. She might ask one student what would happen to the world if 2 plus 2 no longer equaled 4. Or she might ask another to name the top ten reasons why giraffes are not allowed on school buses.

One morning when the students got to school, they found Mrs. Dibble studying four sealed boxes.

This time the students had a question for Mrs. Dibble. "What's in the boxes?" they asked.

Mrs. Dibble's response wasn't exactly what the students were expecting.

"Well, these boxes have been in the storage closet so long I can't remember what they contain," answered Mrs. Dibble. "But here's what I do know:

"If you square the weight of Box 1, it equals the weight of Box 2.
"If you square the weight of Box 2, it equals the weight of Box 4.
"The weight of Box 3 is a multiple of Boxes 1 and 2 and a factor of Box 4.
"If you add the weights of all four boxes, you get 120 pounds.

"So," continued Mrs. Dibble, "if you can tell me the weight of each box, I'll be able to remember what's inside each one!"

Now It's Your Turn
Use the clues to figure out the weight of each box. Then describe the mathematical pattern represented by the 4 weights.

Bonus Box: If Box 1 weighed 4 pounds and the first three clues stayed the same, what would the total weight of the boxes be?

Giving and Getting

Finding the dollar amount that will yield $50.00 for charity with some left over

Teacher Page

Problem-solving strategies

students could use:
- guess and check
- make a list, table, or chart
- choose the correct operation

Math skills

students will use:
- identify, extend, and use patterns
- make and test predictions
- understand and use percents
- multiply decimals
- round to the nearest dollar

Restating the problem: Amelia learns a lesson about percents when her mom offers her a deal. Each month her mom will give her between $1.00 and $100.00, but whatever amount is given, that percent will be given to charity. For example, if given $75.00, Amelia will give 75% to charity. What amount will allow Amelia to give about $50.00 to charity and still have some left over for spending money?

Important information found in the problem:
- Amelia's mom agrees to give her between $1.00 and $100.00 each month.
- Part of that money will be for Amelia to keep. The other part will be for charity.
- The dollar amount of the money determines the percentage that must be given to charity. For example, if Amelia gets $10.00, then 10% of $10.00 goes to charity.
- Amelia wants to give about $50.00 a month to charity and still have some money left for herself.

Answer Key There are two possible answers. If Amelia's mom gives her $70.00, she can give $49.00 to charity. If her mom gives her $71.00, Amelia can give $50.41 to charity.

Bonus Box answer: It will take 18 weeks for Lil to have more savings than Amelia.

Helpful Hints

Share this information when students get stuck to help put them back on the path to correctly solving the problem.

Hint 1 Make a four-column chart as shown.

Allowance	Percent for Charity	Amount for Charity	Amount for Amelia

Hint 2 In the first column, list the given amounts: $1.00, $10.00, $75.00. In the second column, list the percents for charity: 1%, 10%, and 75%. To find the amount for charity, multiply the allowance by the decimal form of the percent. List the answer in the third column. To find the amount for Amelia, subtract the amount for charity from the allowance. Then list the answer in the fourth column.

Hint 3 Study the chart to find the monthly amount that will give about $50.00 to charity. Notice that $75.00 is too much. Guess and check to find the dollar amount closest to $50.00.

Giving and Getting

Amelia cares about the problems of the world. She cares about people who don't have enough food. She cares about preventing pollution. She cares about dogs and cats in shelters waiting for good homes.

So every week when her mom gives her a few dollars, Amelia can't decide how to use it. She wonders, "Should I spend it on a CD or give it to the Red Cross? Help save a tree or get an ice-cream cone after school?"

Amelia's mom noticed her problem and decided to help her figure out a way to be generous and still have some spending money left. She offered Amelia a deal.

"Each month I'll give you any amount between $1.00 and $100.00," she proposed.

Amelia's face lit up.

"But whatever amount I give you," Mom continued, "you'll give a certain percentage of it to the charity of your choice. Here's how it'll work: If I give you $1.00, you'll give 1% of it to charity. If I give you $10.00, you'll give 10% of it to charity. If I give you $75.00, you'll give 75% of it to charity."

Amelia gave this some thought. "What amount between $1.00 and $100.00 would allow me to give about $50.00 a month to charity and still have some spending money left for myself?" she wondered.

Now It's Your Turn
Figure out how much money Amelia should ask her mom to give her each month. Remember: She wants to give about $50.00 a month to charity and still have some left for spending money.

Bonus Box: Amelia and her sister, Lil, decide to increase the amount of money they each have in their piggy banks. Amelia will start with $75.00 and add $3.00 each week. Lil will start with $40.00 and add $5.00 each week. How many weeks will it take for Lil to have more money saved than Amelia?

Candle-Burning Mystery

Calculating the length of candles burning at different rates

Problem-solving strategies

students could use:

- guess and check
- make a list, table, or chart
- find a pattern

Math skills

students will use:

- identify, extend, and use patterns
- calculate rates
- simplify fractions
- determine elapsed time
- find a fractional part of a number

Restating the problem: The electricity in the house goes out at 10:00 P.M., and two candles are lit. The eight-inch candle will burn for four hours. The ten-inch candle will burn for ten hours. When will the shorter candle be exactly half the length of the other? When will the longer candle be 5³/₄ inches long?

Important information found in the problem:
- At 10:00 P.M. two candles, a dinner candle and an emergency candle, are lit.
- The dinner candle is eight inches long and will burn for four hours.
- The emergency candle is ten inches long and will burn for ten hours.

Answer Key The dinner candle will be half the length of the emergency candle at midnight. The emergency candle will be 5³/₄ inches long at 2:15 A.M.

Bonus Box answer: The third candle will be half melted at 4:00 A.M. and completely melted at 10:00 A.M.

Helpful Hints

Share this information when students get stuck to help put them back on the path to correctly solving the problem.

Hint 1 Determine the rate at which each candle is burning. If the dinner candle burns eight inches in four hours, represent it with the fraction ⁸/₄, which reduces to ²/₁, or two inches per hour. If the emergency candle burns ten inches in ten hours, represent it with ¹⁰/₁₀, which reduces to ¹/₁, or one inch per hour.

Hint 2 Make a table with column headings for time, length of dinner candle, and length of emergency candle. Complete the table, using each candle's burn-rate pattern. Study the table to see that the emergency candle is six inches long at 2:00 A.M. and five inches long at 3:00 A.M. To find out when it will be 5³/₄ inches long, calculate the number of minutes in three-fourths of an hour *(45 minutes)*. Subtract 45 minutes from 3:00 A.M. to determine when the candle will be that length *(2:15 A.M.)*.

Candle-Burning Mystery

It's finally here!

Like many other kids, Donna and Daniel Reed could hardly wait for the day when the fifth book in their favorite mystery series would arrive. On the big day, the whole family stood in a long line outside the bookstore until they were able to purchase two copies.

That night, dinner was served early. Dishes were cleared and washed in a flash. Donna and Daniel didn't even think about TV. They started reading right away.

They were so absorbed in their books that they didn't notice the sounds of a thunderstorm outside. Then, all of a sudden, the lights went out!

Quickly, the family gathered in the living room. They lit 2 candles: a dinner candle and an emergency candle. Donna and Daniel tried to keep reading by the candlelight, but they were not happy.

Sensing the kids' growing disappointment, their father offered a mathematical puzzle for them to solve. "It's 10:00 P.M., and we've just lit 2 candles," he said. "The dinner candle is 8 inches tall and will burn for 4 hours. The emergency candle is 10 inches tall and will burn for 10 hours. At what time will the shorter candle be exactly half the length of the longer candle? And at what time will the emergency candle be $5\frac{3}{4}$ inches long?"

Donna and Daniel now had a *real* mystery to solve!

Now It's Your Turn

Figure out when the dinner candle will be half as long as the emergency candle and when the emergency candle with be $5\frac{3}{4}$ inches long.

Bonus Box: Donna and Daniel find a third candle. It is 6 inches tall and will burn for 12 hours. At what time will it be half melted? Completely melted?

A Teacher Who Really Measures Up!

POW! #17

Converting three different units of linear measurement

Teacher Page

Problem-solving strategies

students could use:
- act it out
- write an equation
- choose the correct operation

Math skills

students will use:
- multiply and divide
- convert units
- write fractions in simplest form
- decide whether an answer is reasonable

standard foot—12 inches
Addison foot—9 inches
Madison foot—7 inches

Restating the problem: Addison Zilch wins his school's Teacher-for-a-Day contest. In his winning essay, he proposes that the standard 12-inch foot be replaced by the nine-inch Addison foot and the seven-inch Madison foot. He gives the class the measurements of four items. What are the measurements of the given items using each unit?

Important information found in the problem:
- Addison Zilch becomes his class's teacher for a day by winning an essay contest.
- His assignment for the students is to convert measurements from standard feet (12 inches) to Addison feet (nine inches) and Madison feet (seven inches).
- Addison provides a list of measurements:
  height of school nurse: $5\frac{1}{2}$ standard feet
  diameter of kickball: $\frac{3}{4}$ standard foot
  height and length of swing set: 10 x 12 Addison feet
  length and width of principal's office: 26 x 20 Madison feet
- Students must give measurements in all three units.

Answer Key Students should make a table similar to the following:

	Standard Feet	Addison Feet	Madison Feet
height of school nurse	$5\frac{1}{2}$	$7\frac{1}{3}$	$9\frac{3}{7}$
diameter of kickball	$\frac{3}{4}$	1	$1\frac{2}{7}$
height and length of swing set	$7\frac{1}{2}$ x 9	10 x 12	$12\frac{6}{7}$ x $15\frac{3}{7}$
length and width of principal's office	$15\frac{1}{6}$ x $11\frac{2}{3}$	$20\frac{2}{9}$ x $15\frac{5}{9}$	26 x 20

Bonus Box answer: Answers will vary. Each student will measure her height and the length of her foot and convert these measurements to Addison and Madison feet.

Helpful Hints
Share this information when students get stuck to help put them back on the path to correctly solving the problem.

Hint 1 Make a nine-inch Addison ruler and a seven-inch Madison ruler. Practice measuring items with them as well as a standard ruler.

Hint 2 The size of an inch stays the same in all three systems. The only change is in the number of inches per foot.

Hint 3 Convert feet to inches by multiplying according to the unit being used. If the original measurement is in standard feet, multiply by 12. For Addison feet, multiply by nine. For Madison feet, multiply by seven. Then divide to convert the inches into the new unit. For standard feet, divide by 12. For Addison feet, divide by nine. For Madison feet, divide by seven.

A Teacher Who Really Measures Up!

POW! #17

To compete in the annual Teacher-for-a-Day contest, students write essays proposing new lesson plans. Each class winner gets to be the teacher for a day.

Students love this contest, but teachers get tired of reading essays that propose the same ideas every year: no homework, longer lunches, and so on.

This year, the teachers agreed that the winners will be those who propose unique ideas. That decision practically guaranteed a win in Ms. Nil's room for Addison Zilch, a whiz kid who reads encyclopedias for fun!

Addison's idea involved measurement. He'd been wondering who had decided that a foot should be 12 inches long when his foot was only 9 inches long. So his essay proposed using the 9-inch Addison foot instead of the 12-inch standard foot.

Addison's best friend, Madison, measured her foot and found it was just 7 inches long.

"No problem," said Addison. "I'll propose we use the 7-inch Madison foot too!"

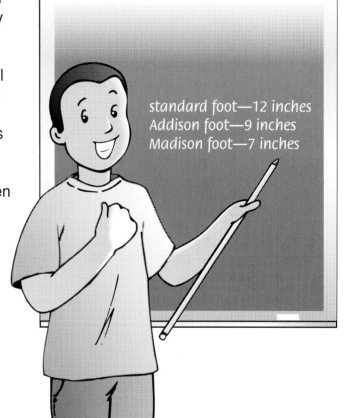

standard foot—12 inches
Addison foot—9 inches
Madison foot—7 inches

Sure enough, Addison won the contest. On his big day, he gave his classmates the following list of measurements:
1. height of school nurse: 5½ standard feet
2. diameter of kickball: ¾ standard foot
3. height and length of swing set: 10 x 12 Addison feet
4. length and width of principal's office: 26 x 20 Madison feet

"Now class, your assignment is to write each measurement in all three units: standard feet, Addison feet, and Madison feet," announced Addison with a satisfied grin. "Wow! It's great being in charge!"

Now It's Your Turn
Make a chart showing each measurement in standard feet, Addison feet, and Madison feet.

Bonus Box: Measure your height and the length of one foot. Make a chart showing both measurements in standard feet, Addison feet, and Madison feet.

Clowning Around

Problem-solving strategies
students could use:

- logical reasoning
- make a list, table, or chart
- guess and check

Math skills
students will use:

- make generalizations
- draw conclusions
- think critically
- make and test predictions

Restating the problem: Three girls join the circus, as do each of their brothers. Because the brothers use clown names instead of real names, no one in their hometown is sure who is who. Which clown is Clara's brother?

Important information found in the problem:
- Dara, Sara, and Clara are friends who become clowns.
- Each girl has a brother who also becomes a clown.
- The brothers use clown names—Chuckles, Wrinkles, and Guffaw—instead of their real names.
- People in Clara's hometown are trying to figure out which clown is her brother.
- In this circus, clowns work in male-female pairs, but no brother works with his sister.
- Chuckles's sister is not Clara.
- Dara refuses to perform with Guffaw because his costume is too similar to hers.
- Sarah's brother is not Wrinkles.
- Wrinkles always performs with Clara.

Answer Key Guffaw is Clara's brother.

Bonus Box answer: Sara performs with Guffaw.

Helpful Hints

Share this information when students get stuck to help put them back on the path to correctly solving the problem.

Hint 1 To use the guess-and-check strategy, pair Clara with each of the male clowns. Then test to see whether the clues are all still true. Keep track of the possibilities.

Hint 2 To use logic, start with the information that Chuckles's sister is not Clara. This makes Clara the sister of either Guffaw or Wrinkles. Then work through the remaining clues until there is only one possibility.

Clowning Around

Clowning around can get you in trouble at school. But if you're trying to join the circus, it's not such a bad idea!

It certainly worked for Clara, who practiced clowning around until she was old enough to join the circus with her friends, Sara and Dara.

In fact, the three girls made clowning around look like such fun that each of their brothers became circus clowns as well! The boys even made up clown names for themselves: Chuckles, Wrinkles, and Guffaw.

Now the circus is coming to perform in Clara's hometown. Posters all around the city advertise the Silly Six: Clara, Sara, Dara, Chuckles, Wrinkles, and Guffaw.

Folks who knew Clara from childhood are trying to figure out which clown is her brother. Is it Chuckles? Or Wrinkles? Or Guffaw? Only the clowns' parents know for sure, and they aren't telling!

A few people actually called circus headquarters, but all they got were these clues:

- In this circus, the clowns always perform in pairs—one female and one male.
- Brothers and sisters don't work together.
- Chuckles's sister is not Clara.
- Dara refuses to perform with Guffaw because his costume is too similar to hers.
- Sara's brother is not Wrinkles.
- Wrinkles always performs with Clara.

Now It's Your Turn

Use the clues to figure out which clown is Clara's brother.

Bonus Box: Using the clues, determine with whom Sara performs.

When 3 and 5 Make 9

Figuring out how to measure nine feet using three feet and five feet

Problem-solving strategies
students could use:

- act it out
- draw a diagram
- guess and check
- choose the correct operation
- make a list, table, or chart

Math skills
students will use:

- estimate sums and differences
- make and test predictions
- use logical reasoning
- use visual representations to solve problems

Restating the problem: Alvin and Jake need to measure a nine-foot length to mark boundaries for a game. How can they do this using only their heights—five feet and three feet—and a very long piece of string?

Important information found in the problem:

- Alvin is five feet tall.
- Jake is three feet tall.
- They invented a game that requires goals to be nine feet apart.
- They do not have any measuring tools to help them, only a very long piece of string.

Answer Key Answers may vary in wording and sequence, but should be similar to the following:

1. On the string, mark Alvin's height (5 feet).
2. On the string, mark Jake's height (3 feet).
3. Compare the marks and then subtract 3 feet from 5 feet. Mark the resulting 2-foot segment.
4. Subtract the 2-foot segment from the 3-foot segment. Mark this 1-foot segment.
5. Add the 5-foot, 3-foot, and 1-foot segments to make 9 feet.

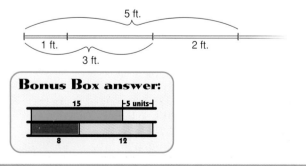

Bonus Box answer:

Helpful Hints

Share this information when students get stuck to help put them back on the path to correctly solving the problem.

Hint 1 Model the problem. Use string to measure, add, and subtract the heights of two students. Fold the string back to show subtraction.

Hint 2 Draw a diagram. Use line segments to represent the different lengths of string. Begin with Alvin's and Jake's heights. Then subtract and add the lengths as needed to determine how to mark the resulting segments.

Hint 3 Make a list of all the different combinations and differences that can be reached, beginning with the two original heights. Look for a combination that totals nine.

When 3 and 5 Make 9

POW! #19

Alvin has a little shadow that follows him around—his little brother, Jake! But that's okay with Alvin, who actually feels pretty lucky to have a brother who's not only good at sports, but is also a bit of a mathematical genius.

Most days after school, Alvin and Jake play baseball, hockey, or basketball. When they get tired of these sports, they make up their own games.

One day, Jake had a moment of inspiration. "Let's get some hollow cardboard tubes and a Ping-Pong ball. We'll put the ball on a center line and try to get the ball in the opposite goal by blowing through the tubes."

"Cool," said Alvin. "How far apart should the goals be?"

"Let's use my lucky number—9," replied Jake.

That was fine with Alvin, except for one thing. They didn't have any way of measuring exactly 9 feet. They emptied their pockets, but all they found was $0.76, 2 sticks of old gum, and a very long piece of string.

That was all Jake needed. "Alvin, we're home free!" he exclaimed. "Listen, you're exactly 5 feet tall. I'm exactly 3 feet tall. We can use this string to measure our heights."

"But Jake," protested Alvin, "5 feet plus 3 feet is not 9 feet."

"Leave it to me," answered the boy genius. "I know how to use 3 and 5 and a little adding and subtracting to make 9!"

Now It's Your Turn
How can Jake use the string and the boys' heights to measure exactly 9 feet?

Bonus Box: On another day, Alvin and Jake found 3 measuring sticks of 8, 12, and 15 units. They used the sticks to measure a length of 5 units. Use the line spaces on a sheet of notebook paper to show how they did this.

Building-Block Math

Finding the number of painted faces when a cube is broken into separate blocks

Teacher Page

Problem-solving strategies
students could use:

- make a list, table, or chart
- find a pattern
- act it out
- solve a simpler problem
- draw a picture

Math skills
students will use:

- identify, extend, and use patterns
- make generalizations
- recognize and continue geometric patterns
- recognize, represent, and visualize solid figures
- use manipulatives

cube	3 painted faces	2 painted faces	1 painted face	no pain face
3 x 3 x 3				
4 x 4 x 4				
5 x 5 x 5				
6 x 6 x 6				

Restating the problem: Tina wants to prove to her mom that her old building blocks and fingerpaints are useful learning toys. She constructs different-sized cubes from the blocks and paints the outside of each one. How many blocks will have three painted faces when the cubes are broken into individual blocks? Two faces? One face? No faces?

Important information found in the problem:
- Tina pastes blocks together to make a 2 x 2 x 2 cube.
- She paints the outside of the 2 x 2 x 2 cube. When she takes it apart, she notices that some of the blocks have one painted face, some have two painted faces, and some have three painted faces.
- She repeats this process with a 3 x 3 x 3 cube, a 4 x 4 x 4 cube, and a 5 x 5 x 5 cube.
- Her mom asks her to make a chart showing the results for each cube and then use the chart's patterns to predict what would happen with a 6 x 6 x 6 cube.

Answer Key Answers should include a chart as shown.

Cube	3 Painted Faces	2 Painted Faces	1 Painted Face	No Painted Faces
3 x 3 x 3	8	12	6	1
4 x 4 x 4	8	24	24	8
5 x 5 x 5	8	36	54	27
6 x 6 x 6	8	48	96	64

Bonus Box answer: In a 7 x 7 x 7 cube, there are eight blocks that have three painted faces, 60 blocks that have two painted faces, 150 blocks that have one painted face, and 125 blocks that have no painted faces.

Helpful Hints

Share this information when students get stuck to help put them back on the path to correctly solving the problem.

Hint 1 Use blocks or interlocking plastic cubes to model the problem. Place four blocks on top of four blocks to construct a 2 x 2 x 2 cube. Imagine that the outside of the cube is painted. Determine the number of faces on each block that would be painted *(3)*.

Hint 2 Construct a 3 x 3 x 3 cube to see that some of its blocks have no painted faces while others have one, two, or three painted faces.

Hint 3 Set up a chart with columns that show the number of blocks that have zero, one, two, or three painted faces. Include rows for a 3 x 3 x 3 cube, a 4 x 4 x 4 cube, a 5 x 5 x 5 cube, and a 6 x 6 x 6 cube.

Hint 4 Notice that the number of blocks having three painted faces always equals eight (for the corners). The column with two painted faces increases by 12. The column with no painted faces follows this pattern: 1^3, 2^3, 3^3, 4^3. To determine the number of blocks with one painted face, first find the total number of blocks in each cube (multiply 3 x 3 x 3, 4 x 4 x 4, 5 x 5 x 5, and 6 x 6 x 6). Then subtract the sum of the other three columns from that product.

Building-Block Math

Tina's mom is usually easygoing, but once a year, she turns into a real cleaning machine!

Tina really doesn't mind tidying her room. She just wishes her mom wouldn't make her give away toys she's outgrown, such as her fingerpaints and wooden building blocks.

With cleaning day approaching, Tina comes up with a plan to prove that she can still learn from her old toys.

cube	3 painted faces	2 painted faces	1 painted face	no painted faces
3 x 3 x 3				
4 x 4 x 4				
5 x 5 x 5				
6 x 6 x 6				

"Mom, I'm going to use my building blocks and fingerpaints to study math," Tina announced. "Watch me paint one block," Tina said, as she smeared blue paint on it. "See how all 6 faces are blue? Now I'm going to paste 8 blocks together to make a cube that's 2 blocks high, 2 blocks long, and 2 blocks wide," Tina continued. She painted the cube and set it aside. When the cube was dry, she broke it apart into its 8 separate blocks.

"Look, Mom!" exclaimed Tina. "Three faces of each block are blue!"

Tina then built a 3 x 3 x 3 cube, a 4 x 4 x 4 cube, and a 5 x 5 x 5 cube. She painted the outside of each one, let it dry, and then broke it apart to determine the number of blocks in each cube with 0, 1, 2, or 3 painted sides.

Mom smiled and said, "Okay, you can keep the blocks *if* you'll make a chart of your results so far and then predict what would happen with a 6 x 6 x 6 cube."

Now It's Your Turn

Make a chart showing the number of painted faces on each block when a 3 x 3 x 3 cube, a 4 x 4 x 4 cube, and a 5 x 5 x 5 cube are taken apart. Use the pattern in each column to predict the number of painted faces you'd find if a 6 x 6 x 6 cube were taken apart.

Bonus Box: Add a row to the chart for a 7 x 7 x 7 cube. Then use the established pattern to complete that row of the chart.

Counting Her Sheep

Finding patterns in the sums of the digits on a digital clock

$8:00 \quad 8+0+0 = 8$
$9:00 \quad 9+0+0 = 9$
$10:00 \quad 1+0+0+0 = 1$

Problem-solving strategies
students could use:
- guess and check
- make a list, table, or chart
- find a pattern

Math skills
students will use:
- draw conclusions
- make and test predictions
- identify, extend, and use patterns
- use number sense

Restating the problem: Little Bo-Peep lies awake one night worrying about her lost sheep. She begins to add the digits on her digital clock and notices a pattern. What pattern emerges between 8:00 P.M. and 11:00 P.M.? What are the greatest and least possible sums of the digits?

Important information found in the problem:
- Little Bo-Peep is having trouble sleeping, so she adds the digits displayed on her digital clock.
- 8:00 P.M. becomes $8 + 0 + 0$ which equals 8, and 8:01 becomes $8 + 0 + 1$ which equals 9.
- She adds the digits, not the numbers. For example, 10:01 becomes $1 + 0 + 0 + 1 = 2$, not $10 + 0 + 1 = 11$.
- She notices that two unique sums occur from 8:00 P.M. to 11:00 P.M.

(Answer Key) The greatest possible sum is 23, occurring at 9:59 P.M. The least possible sum is 1, occurring at 10:00 P.M.

Bonus Box answer: Answers will vary. Possible answers include the following.
1. At 8:00, the sum is 8. At 9:00, it is 9. But at 10:00, the sum is 1. At 11:00, the pattern continues with a sum of 2.
2. The sum increases by 1 for each successive minute past the hour.
3. At each 10-minute increment, the pattern repeats, starting with the next counting number. For example, 8:10—9, 8:20—10, 8:30—11, etc. But at 10:00, it starts with a sum of 1 and then continues the same pattern.
4. At 8:59, the sum is 22. At 9:59, it is 23. But at 10:59, the sum is 15, and the pattern starts repeating again.

Helpful Hints

Share this information when students get stuck to help put them back on the path to correctly solving the problem.

Hint 1 Remember that 8:00 is counted as $8 + 0 + 0$, 9:00 is counted as $9 + 0 + 0$, and 10:00 is counted as $1 + 0 + 0 + 0$.

Hint 2 Make a chart with columns for the minutes (:00 through :59) and the hours of 8:00, 9:00, and 10:00 as shown. Then complete the chart by filling in the sums.

minutes	8:00	9:00	10:00
:00	8	9	1
:01	9	10	2
:02	10	11	3
:03	11	12	4

Hint 3 Look for a pattern in the chart's rows and columns, looking especially at the greatest and least possible sums within each hour.

Counting Her Sheep

Little Bo-Peep
Lost her sheep
And didn't know where to find them.
She worried a heap
And couldn't sleep,
So she added numbers instead
of counting sheep.

If you think that poem is bad, you should try losing all your sheep! Little Bo-Peep was very worried about going to work the next day and telling her boss that the flock had fled.

So you can bet she didn't try counting her sheep to get to sleep. Instead, as she watched the minutes tick away on her digital clock, she began to think about the sum of the numbers.

"8:00 P.M., 8:01 P.M. What would happen if I added the digits? Hmmm...
$8 + 0 + 0 = 8$, and $8 + 0 + 1 = 9$."

Then the clock changed to 8:02. "Wow, now the sum is 10! This is pretty interesting," she thought.

Bo-Peep continued to add all the times from 8:00 P.M. to 11:00 P.M. She discovered that different times sometimes result in the same sum. For example, 9:29 and 8:48 both total 20. And she found the greatest and least possible sums.

Now It's Your Turn

Find the pattern that results from adding the digits on a digital clock from 8:00 P.M. to 11:00 P.M. What are the greatest and least possible sums? At what times do they occur?

Bonus Box: Describe the pattern that occurs between 8:00 P.M. and 11:00 P.M. when adding the digits on a digital clock.

X-tra, X-tra!

Solving a magic square that contains an unknown variable

Problem-solving strategies

students could use:

- guess and check
- write an equation
- draw a picture or diagram

Math skills

students will use:

- make and test predictions
- find the value of an unknown variable
- write and evaluate algebraic expressions
- combine like terms in an algebraic equation

Restating the problem: Newsboy Albert E. puts math problems in the newspapers he sells. One day he adds a magic square that contains the variable x. What number does x represent in the square?

Important information found in the problem:
- Albert E., a math-loving newsboy, says "X-tra, x-tra!" instead of "Extra, extra!" because he loves to use math variables.
- He puts math problems in the newspapers he sells.
- His latest edition contains a 3 x 3 magic square in which each column, row, and diagonal results in the same sum.
- Four of the magic square's boxes contain the variable x. The x represents the same number throughout the square.

Answer Key $x = 7$

Bonus Box answer: Answers may vary. The sum of each row, column, and diagonal in the magic square should be the same. One possible puzzle:

8	1	6
3	5	7
4	9	2

Helpful Hints

Share this information when students get stuck to help put them back on the path to correctly solving the problem.

Hint 1 Rows are horizontal, columns are vertical, and diagonals go from one corner to the opposite corner through the center.

Hint 2 The variable x must represent the same number each time it is used. However, the resulting number in each square will depend on the number that is added to or subtracted from x. For example, if $x = 5$, then the square containing the expression $x + 5$ is equal to 10.

Hint 3 Focus on making any two rows, columns, or diagonals equal by guessing and checking. When you find a number that works for those two groupings, try using it in the rest of the problem.

Hint 4 Write an equation to solve the problem. Using any two rows, columns, or diagonals, set one equal to the other and then solve for x. For example, to set Row 1 equal to Row 2, use the equation $(x + 5) + (x - 2) + 10 = 7 + 9 + (x + 4)$. Combine like terms and then solve for x to find the answer.

$$2x + 5 - 2 + 10 = 7 + 9 + x + 4$$
$$2x + 13 = 20 + x$$
$$2x = 7 + x$$
$$x = 7$$

X-tra, X-tra!

POW! #22

Back in the 1860s, folks didn't have computers, TVs, or radios.

So how did they find out about important events, such as which side was winning the Civil War? They rushed outside to buy the latest newspaper! Whenever there was a hot news flash, newsboys would stand on corners yelling, "Extra, extra! Read all about it!"

Well, that's what most newsboys would yell. Newsboy Albert E. was an exception.

When Albert E. stood on a corner, he didn't yell, "Extra, extra!" He yelled, "X-tra, x-tra!" And when he mentioned *x*, he meant a variable.

A variable, you ask? An unknown number? The kind you have to solve for in equations? Yep, that's right!

Most of the time, Albert E. was content just to say "X-tra" instead of "Extra." But once in awhile, he would add math puzzles to his stack of newspapers. The problem one day was a magic square.

In a magic square, you get the same sum when you add each column, row, and diagonal. So all you really have to do is add and, of course, figure out what number *x* represents.

Now It's Your Turn
Find the number that *x* must represent to give the same sum in every row, column, and diagonal. Remember: The variable *x* represents the same number throughout the magic square. For example, if *x* equals 100 in the top left box, then it equals 100 everywhere in the puzzle.

Bonus Box: You don't have to be Albert E. to create a magic square. Try to find another set of nine numbers that add up to the same sum in all directions. You don't have to use a variable.

Does That Compute?

Using letters to represent numbers in mathematical operations

$A = 1, B = 2, C = 3,$
$D = 4, E = 5, F = 6$

Problem-solving strategies
students could use:

- guess and check
- make a list, table, or chart
- logical reasoning

Math skills
students will use:

- find the multiples of a number
- find the least common multiple
- find the greatest common factor
- distinguish between primes and composites
- make and test predictions
- understand inequalities
- solve equations

ONE-A

Restating the problem: Because of faulty wiring, robot One-A uses numbers for writing and letters for math. One-A's inventors give up on the robot and send it to school, where it poses strange questions to the teacher. Using One-A's system, can you answer its questions?

Important information found in the problem:
- In One-A's system, each letter equals a different number. A = 1, B = 2, C = 3, and so on.
- All of One-A's questions are based on this system.
- Words have the numerical value of the sum of their letters.

Answer Key

1. Answers will vary. Possible words using multiples of 5 include *toy, joy, jet, yet, jot,* and *toe.*
2. The LCM of B (2) and K (11) is V (22).
3. The GCF of H (8) and T (20) is D (4).
4. The letters that represent prime numbers are B (2), C (3), E (5), G (7), K (11), M (13), Q (17), S (19), and W (23).
5. Answers will vary. However, the blank must be filled in using a word (or words) that has a value greater than 74. Possible answers include KETCHUP (84) or PIZZA (78).

Bonus Box answer: Answers will vary but must include the numerical value of the sum of the first name's letters and an adjective with the same numerical value.

Helpful Hints

Share this information when students get stuck to help put them back on the path to correctly solving the problem.

Hint 1 List each letter with its corresponding number to use as a reference.

Hint 2 A *multiple* of a number is the product of that number and another factor.

Hint 3 The *least common multiple* (LCM) of two numbers is the smallest number that is a multiple of both.

Hint 4 The *greatest common factor* (GCF) of two numbers is the largest number that is a factor of both.

Hint 5 A *prime number* is a number greater than one that has only two factors: itself and one.

Does That Compute?

POW! #23

Some folks believe that robots may one day take over all the boring jobs that humans don't want to do. Sounds great, doesn't it? But technology hasn't gotten that far yet at Mom and Pop's Robot Shop.

You see, Mom and Pop couldn't agree on how One-A, their latest invention, should be programmed. Mom thought One-A should be a mathematical genius, so she started filling its circuits with numbers. Pop thought One-A should be a literary genius, so he started filling its circuits with letters.

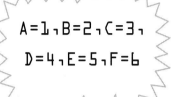

A = 1, B = 2, C = 3, D = 4, E = 5, F = 6

Unfortunately, because of faulty wiring, the numbers and letters got all jumbled up in One-A's database. As a result, it uses letters to do math and numbers to write words. One-A's first sentence, for example, was EGGS + TOAST < MY BREAKFAST.

Mom and Pop puzzled for a long time until they figured out that if A = 1, B = 2, and so on, then EGGS (38) plus TOAST (75) was less than MY BREAKFAST (121).

"Eight less," added One-A, with a mechanical chuckle. Mom and Pop didn't understand the robot's sense of humor until they figured out that "eight less" sounds just like "ate less."

"This robot is useless and has a terrible sense of humor," declared Pop.

"You're right," agreed Mom. "Let's send it to school. Maybe it will learn something."

But One-A didn't learn a thing. It just kept asking the teacher crazy questions, which she would then assign to her students.

Now It's Your Turn
Using One-A's system of A = 1, B = 2, and so on, answer the following questions:
1. **Using multiples of 5, write 5 words.**
2. **What letter is the least common multiple of B and K?**
3. **What letter is the greatest common factor of H and T?**
4. **List all of the letters that represent prime numbers in One-A's alphabet.**
5. **Complete the inequality below. It must be mathematically correct and also make sense.**

HAMBURGER + _____ > VERY DELICIOUS

Hint: Read this sentence as "Hamburger plus blank is more than very delicious."

Bonus Box: Calculate the numerical value of your first, middle, or last name. Then write a word that describes you and has the same numerical value as your name.

Tutoring Tactics

Finding a common multiple of three numbers

Problem-solving strategies
students could use:
- make a list, chart, or table
- find a pattern
- act it out

Math skills
students will use:
- identify and extend patterns
- generate multiples
- find common multiples
- find the fraction of a number

Restating the problem: Roger wants to make as much money as possible tutoring three children. Each child has a different study pattern. For him to earn the most money, the children must all be studying at the same time when their parents return. What time between noon and 1:00 P.M. should Roger have the parents come home?

Important information found in the problem:
- The tutoring session begins at 9:00 A.M. and ends between noon and 1:00 P.M.
- Roger will make the most money if all three children are studying at the time the parents return home.
- Hank studies for half an hour and relaxes for ten minutes.
- Amelia studies for three-quarters of an hour and relaxes for five minutes.
- Julia studies for five minutes and relaxes for a quarter of an hour.

Answer Key All 3 children will be studying at the following times: 12:00 noon–12:05 P.M., 12:20 P.M.–12:25 P.M., and 12:40 P.M.–12:45 P.M.

Bonus Box answer: Answers may vary.

Helpful Hints

Hint 1 Change all times from fractions of an hour to minutes.

Hint 2 Make a timetable for each child starting at 9:00 A.M. and ending at 1:00 P.M.

Hint 3 Focus on the period between noon and 1:00 P.M.

Hint 4 Look for common five-minute periods.

Hint 5 Look for a pattern of multiples. Hank's pattern repeats every 40 minutes, Amelia's every 50 minutes, and Julia's every 20 minutes. Find the least common multiple of these three numbers *(200).* Add that number of minutes to 9:00 A.M. to find one of the three times they'll all begin working again at the same time.

Tutoring Tactics

Roger has a serious problem. Not a school problem—he's a straight A student. Not a home problem—he gets along well with his parents. Not a social problem—he has plenty of friends. So what's Roger's problem? Money! He desperately wants $60.00 to buy the latest computer game.

That's why Roger agreed to take a job tutoring the 3 Dillingham children on Saturday morning. What Roger didn't realize was that tutoring the Dillingham children would be like conducting a three-ring circus!

On Saturday morning, Mrs. Dillingham explained to Roger that all 3 children must start studying at 9:00 A.M. "Hank will study for half an hour and then relax for 10 minutes. Amelia will study for three-quarters of an hour and then relax for 5 minutes. Julia will study for 5 minutes and then relax for a quarter of an hour. When Mr. Dillingham and I return home, we will decide how much to pay you. You'll get $20.00 for each child who is studying the moment we arrive."

Roger didn't know whether to laugh or cry. "Do you mean I could make $60.00 or nothing?"

"That's right," answered Mrs. Dillingham. "But to be fair, we'll let *you* decide when you want us to be home between noon and 1:00 P.M."

Now It's Your Turn

Help Roger figure out the times between noon and 1:00 P.M. that all 3 Dillingham children will be studying at the same time.

Bonus Box: Create a similar situation and problem for Roger to solve. Be sure to include the answer.

It's a Piece of Cake!

Dividing a cake into 11 pieces with four cuts and 16 pieces with five cuts

Problem-solving strategies

students could use:

- draw a picture
- guess and check
- find a pattern
- make a list, table, or chart

Math skills

students will use:

- identify and extend patterns
- make and test predictions
- use visual representations
- use an input/output table

Restating the problem: A lazy baker is trying to figure out how to cut a round cake into 11 pieces with four cuts and 16 pieces with five cuts.

Important information found in the problem:
- The cake is round.
- The baker can make two pieces with one cut, four pieces with two cuts, and seven pieces with three cuts.
- All cuts must be straight lines.
- The pieces can be different sizes and shapes.

Answer Key

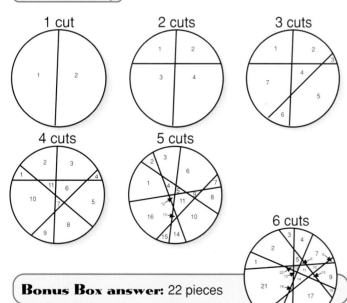

Bonus Box answer: 22 pieces

Helpful Hints

Share this information when students get stuck to help put them back on the path to correctly solving the problem.

Hint 1 Draw a large circle to represent the cake. Use a pencil to draw a line representing each cut.

Hint 2 The cuts will be chords.

Hint 3 Never have more than two cuts intersect at the same point.

Hint 4 Create an input/output table and look for a pattern in the number of cuts (input) and the number of pieces created (output).

It's a Piece of Cake!

POW! #25

The birthday cake specialist at the neighborhood bakery is a very lazy man. Except for licking the bowls, he hardly ever lifts a finger. The baker has machines to do most of the measuring, sifting, mixing, and cleaning. But the baker doesn't have a machine to slice the cakes. He actually has to cut them himself! "This won't do," said the baker. "It's too much work."

So he thought and thought about how to get the most slices from a round cake with the least amount of effort. Finally, he had it!

"Hmmmm…with one straight cut across the cake, I can make 2 pieces. If I make a second cut that crosses the first at some point, I'll have 4 pieces. They won't be equal pieces, of course, but I'll let the kids argue about who gets the biggest slice. A third cut, if done right, can make 7 pieces of cake."

Unfortunately, the baker fell asleep before he could figure out how to make 11 pieces with his fourth cut and 16 pieces with his fifth cut.

Now It's Your Turn
Help this lazy baker by figuring out how to get 11 pieces of cake with 4 cuts and 16 pieces with 5 cuts. Remember that each cut must be a straight line. Include a sketch of the cake in your answer.

Bonus Box: How many slices can the baker make with 6 cuts? Include a drawing that shows the cuts with your answer.

Camp Winniwig's Challenge

Calculating distance, rate, and time

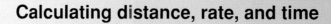

Problem-solving strategies
students could use:

- draw a picture or diagram
- act it out
- guess and check
- work backward
- write an equation

Math skills
students will use:

- use a formula
- use units of time
- convert units of time
- add fractions

Restating the problem: The Miniwig campers try to win the respect of the older Bigwig campers in a bicycle race. Susan, a Miniwig, rides slow and steady while Ben, a Bigwig, rides faster but stops for breaks. The race ends in a tie. How much time does the race take? What is the distance of the race? What is Susan's rate of speed?

Important information found in the problem:
- Susan rides at a constant speed the entire race.
- Ben rides 15 miles per hour for one hour and then stops for 45 minutes.
- Ben rides 15 miles per hour for 30 minutes and then stops for 15 minutes.
- Ben rides 15 miles per hour for 30 minutes to finish the race.
- Susan and Ben finish at the same time.

Answer Key Time—three hours, distance—30 miles, Susan's rate of speed—ten miles per hour

Bonus Box answer: 30 minutes

Helpful Hints

Share this information when students get stuck to help put them back on the path to correctly solving the problem.

Hint 1 Find Ben's total time first. Convert each hour or fractional part of an hour to minutes: 1 hour (60 minutes) + 45 minutes + $1/2$ hour (30 minutes) + 15 minutes + 30 minutes = 3 hours. Since Ben and Susan end the race at the same time, her time is also three hours.

Hint 2 Use the formula *distance = rate x time* to find the distance of each leg of Ben's ride. Then add the lengths to get the total distance traveled.

Hint 3 Use the formula *distance = rate x time* and the race's total time *(three hours)* an distance *(30 miles)* to find Susan's rate of speed.

Camp Winniwig's Challenge

Poor Miniwig bunkmates! Just last summer they were hotshots at junior camp and the rest of the campers looked up to them as if they were movie stars. But this summer they moved up to Camp Winniwig where they aren't feeling so big anymore. "Look at those Bigwig campers!" exclaimed Susan. "They're huge! They're loud! They'll win all the games!"

And to make matters worse, the Bigwigs ignored the Miniwigs. That is, until Susan got their attention with a challenge.

"Hey, you Bigwigs! You may be bigger, stronger, and cooler than us, but I'll bet we're as good as you are at lots of things," announced Susan.

"Oh yeah?" sneered Ben, a Bigwig. "Name one!"

"Ummm…bicycle riding. I bet I could beat any Bigwig in a bicycle race," responded Susan.

"Oh, really?" said Ben. "Well, you're on!"

The whole camp turned out to watch the big race. Susan set off at a steady pace and never slowed down or stopped. Ben rode for an hour at 15 miles per hour and then stopped at the pool for 45 minutes. He rode at 15 miles per hour for another half an hour and stopped for a 15-minute ice-cream break. Finally, he rode 15 miles per hour for another 30 minutes and came to the finish line at exactly the same moment as Susan. The race was a tie!

Now It's Your Turn

Using the formula *distance = rate x time,* figure out how long the race lasted, the distance of the race, and Susan's rate of speed.

Bonus Box: A brother and sister left their house at the same time. The brother headed east on his bicycle riding 13 miles per hour. The sister headed west on her skateboard riding 5 miles per hour. How long will it take them to be 9 miles apart?

We All Scream for Ice Cream

 #27 Finding different arrangements and combinations of variables

Teacher Page

Problem-solving strategies
students could use:
- draw a picture or diagram
- make a list, table, or chart
- find a pattern
- guess and check

Math skills
students will use:
- identify, extend, and use patterns
- list possible combinations
- use permutations

Restating the problem: The 88 students in Mr. Jimmies's class all want different combinations of chocolate and vanilla ice-cream scoops. How many scoops must be on each cone to have at least 88 different cones?

Important information found in the problem:
- There are 88 students in the class.
- Mr. Jimmies is offering two flavors of ice cream: chocolate and vanilla.
- Each student wants a different combination of scoops.
- A double scoop of ice cream yields four possible arrangements.

Answer Key

Scoops	Patterns
1	2
2	4
3	8
4	16
5	32
6	64
7	128

Mr. Jimmies must offer 7 scoops of ice cream per cone.

Bonus Box answer: 27 possible arrangements

CCC	SSS	VVV
CVV	SCC	VCC
CSS	SVV	VSS
CSV	SVC	VCS
CVS	SCV	VSC
CCV	SSV	VVC
CCS	SSC	VVS
CSC	SVS	VCV
CVC	SCS	VSV

Helpful Hints

Share this information when students get stuck to help put them back on the path to correctly solving the problem.

Hint 1 Draw a picture or diagram using symbols for chocolate and vanilla.

Hint 2 Look for a pattern in the number of scoops and the number of possible arrangements of scoops.

Hint 3 A *permutation* is any arrangement of a set of items in which order matters. When the order of the items is changed, a new permutation is created. For example, there are six permutations using the first three letters of the alphabet (*ABC, BCA, BAC, CBA, ACB, CAB*).

Space Crawl

It's a long ride to outer space. And it seems even longer if you spend the whole time worrying about what you'll have to do once you arrive at your destination!

But astronaut Venus D. Milo was a well-known worrywart, so her fellow astronauts weren't too surprised by her behavior during the flight.

"Isn't that just like Venus?" commented one. "She hasn't once looked at the great view of Earth from here."

"She hasn't even tried floating around the cabin to see what it's like without gravity," added another.

The other astronauts went over to ask Venus what she was so worried about. She explained that she was worried about getting out to the satellite to make the repairs.

"Once the spaceship reaches the satellite, I'll have to crawl along a 3 x 3 square grid to get to it. I'll start in the grid's lower left corner. Then, clutching tightly to the grid's bars, I'll crawl to its upper right corner to reach the satellite. I can go only up or to the right—never to the left, down, or diagonally. And if I let go of a bar, I could float off into space!"

And so she was fretting about which route to take.

"There are so many ways to get from the bottom left corner to the upper right corner!" she cried.

No matter how hard the other astronauts tried to convince her to relax, Venus still insisted on figuring out all of the possible routes.

Now It's Your Turn
Use the grid on this page (or copy it onto another sheet of paper) to figure out how many possible routes Venus can take. Remember that she can go only up or to the right—never to the left, down, or diagonally.

Bonus Box: Once Venus figured out all of the possible routes, she decided to take the shortest path. What discovery did she make?

Three on a Trampoline

Calculating what part of a trampoline each child owns

Problem-solving strategies
students could use:

- work backward
- guess and check
- draw a picture or diagram
- act it out

Math skills
students will use:

- find a percent of a number
- convert fractions, percents, and decimals
- use variables
- write and solve an equation

- add fractions with unlike denominators
- use repeating decimals
- construct a circle graph
- use manipulatives

Restating the problem: Three boys buy a trampoline together but they each contribute different amounts of money. What fraction, percent, and decimal of the trampoline is owned by Norbert?

Important information found in the problem:
- Herbert, Norbert, and Schubert put their money together to buy a trampoline.
- Herbert paid for half of the trampoline.
- Norbert paid twice as much as Schubert.
- Herbert owns $\frac{1}{2}$, 50%, or 0.5 of the trampoline.
- The trampoline's cost and the amount of the boys' contributions are not known.

Answer Key Norbert's share is $\frac{1}{3}$, $33\frac{1}{3}$%, or $0.\overline{33}$.

Bonus Box answer: The circle should be divided into 3 sections, representing $\frac{1}{2}$ (Herbert), $\frac{1}{3}$ (Norbert), and $\frac{1}{6}$ (Schubert). To check, measure with a protractor the three central angles: Herbert's section—180°, Norbert's—120°, and Schubert's—60°.

Helpful Hints

Share this information when students get stuck to help put them back on the path to correctly solving the problem.

Hint 1 Make up an amount of money that the trampoline might cost (a multiple of six works well because six is the common denominator of $\frac{1}{2}$, $\frac{1}{3}$, and $\frac{1}{6}$). Subtract half for Herbert. Then divide the remaining amount, giving $\frac{2}{3}$ to Norbert and $\frac{1}{3}$ to Schubert (since Norbert paid twice as much as Schubert). This could be acted out with manipulatives, such as counters, or by drawing a line segment on graph paper.

Hint 2 Once Norbert's fraction is determined, convert it to a decimal by dividing the numerator by the denominator.

Hint 3 Convert the decimal to a percent by multiplying it by 100 or by moving the decimal point two places to the right.

Hint 4 Represent repeating decimals with a bar drawn over the repeating number. For example, $0.\overline{33}$.

Three on a Trampoline

POW! #29

Herbert, Norbert, and Schubert have been best friends ever since they discovered an amazing coincidence: All 3 share a birthday! An even more amazing coincidence is that they were each looking forward to getting the same thing for their birthdays this year.

Their birthday fell on the weekend. But on Monday, all 3 boys came to school with grim faces.

"What's wrong, Herbert?" asked Norbert.

"I didn't get a trampoline for my birthday," replied Herbert. "I only got money."

"I didn't get a trampoline either," chimed in Schubert, "and that's all I really wanted. I got a bunch of gift certificates for a sporting goods store instead."

"I can't believe it," declared Norbert. "That's exactly what happened to me—money and gift certificates, but no trampoline!"

They all agreed that the birthday weekend they'd looked forward to had been a dud. Then Norbert, who was pretty good with numbers, came up with a brilliant idea. "Let's put our money and gift certificates together and buy a trampoline to share!"

Since the boys had received different amounts for their birthdays, Herbert paid for half of the trampoline and Norbert paid twice as much as Schubert. Everyone was satisfied, except for Norbert, who liked to keep the numbers straight.

"It's clear that Herbert owns $\frac{1}{2}$, or 50%, or 0.5 of the trampoline," announced Norbert, "but what fraction, percent, and decimal part of it belongs to me?"

Now It's Your Turn

What part of the trampoline does Norbert own? Write your answer as a fraction, a decimal, and a percent.

Bonus Box: Use a compass (or trace a round object, such as a can) to construct a circle graph representing the trampoline. Divide the circle into sections that show exactly how much of the trampoline each boy owns. Label each corresponding section of the graph with the correct boy's name.

Escape From the Zoo

Determining whether a zebra or a zookeeper will reach a gate first

Problem-solving strategies
students could use:
- make a list, table, or chart
- draw a picture
- solve a simpler problem
- find a pattern
- write an equation

Math skills
students will use:
- convert miles per hour to feet per minute
- multiply four-digit numbers
- use a calculator to divide by multiple-digit divisors
- calculate elapsed time

Restating the problem: The exit door to the zoo was accidentally left open. An escaped zebra and a zookeeper are running toward the open exit gate. Will the zookeeper reach the exit in time to prevent the zebra from escaping?

Important information found in the problem:
- The zebra is running 40 mph and is one mile from the exit.
- The zookeeper is running ten mph and is 880 feet from the exit.
- The problem asks students to figure out who will get to the exit first: the zebra or the zookeeper.

Answer Key It will take the zebra 1 minute and 30 seconds to get to the exit. It will take the zookeeper 1 minute to get to the exit. The zookeeper will get there first.

Bonus Box answer: The human will run 15 miles per hour (60 ÷ 4). Fastest to slowest order— elephant, human, squirrel.

Helpful Hints
Share this information when students get stuck to help put them back on the path to correctly solving the problem.

Hint 1 Draw a diagram that shows the zebra one mile from the exit and the zookeeper 880 feet from the exit. Convert miles to feet so the zebra's and zookeeper's distances will be in the same unit of measure *(1 mile = 5,280 feet).*

Hint 2 Find the difference in speeds per minute. The zebra runs 40 mph or 211,200 feet per hour, which is 3,520 feet per minute. The zookeeper runs ten mph or 52,800 feet per hour, which is 880 feet per minute.

Hint 3 If the zebra runs 3,520 feet per minute, figure out how many minutes it will take it to run 5,280 feet to the exit *(5,280 ÷ 3,520 = 1 minute 30 seconds).* If the zookeeper runs 880 feet in one minute, figure out how many minutes it will take him to run 880 feet *(1 minute).*

Escape From the Zoo

Walking through the zoo, the last thing you would expect to see is a zebra and a zookeeper running for the exit. But that is just what happened last Saturday!

My brother and I were walking through the zoo, looking at all the different animals and eating popcorn. Jeb was trying to imitate a gorilla when all of a sudden a zebra ran by us! We looked around and saw that someone had left its cage open.

"Quick! Someone call the main office. A zebra has escaped!" I yelled.

A lady near us pulled out her cell phone and started dialing. I don't know who she was calling, but it didn't matter because from the other direction, we could see the zookeeper heading for the exit gate.

That's when I realized that the gate leading out of the park—you know, the one with "Exit" written above it in bright red letters—was wide open. And the zebra was running straight for it!!

Would the zookeeper get there in time to close and lock the exit gate? Or would the zebra escape?

Now It's Your Turn
The zebra is running 40 mph and is 1 mile from the exit. The zookeeper is running 10 mph and is 880 feet from the exit. Will the zebra escape before the zookeeper reaches the gate?

Bonus Box: An elephant's top speed is about 25 mph, a squirrel can run about 12 mph, and a fast human runner can run 1 mile in about 4 minutes. Convert the human's speed into miles per hour. Then list the 3 speeds in order from fastest to slowest.

Note to the teacher: Allow students to use calculators to solve this problem.

One-Wheeled Wanderings

Using a number line to find the distance between opposite integers

Teacher Page

Problem-solving strategies
students could use:
- draw a picture or diagram
- choose the correct operation
- write an equation
- act it out

Math skills
students will use:
- use a number line to calculate
- add and subtract integers
- write number sentences with integers

Restating the problem: Lila practices riding her unicycle each day by going forward and backward on a 100-foot path. How many feet does she ride each day?

Important information found in the problem:
- Lila rides her unicycle the same distance each day.
- Her path is 100 feet long and marked in ten-foot intervals.
- The midpoint of the path is marked 0. The intervals to the right of 0 are marked 10, 20, 30, 40, and 50. The intervals to the left of 0 are marked ‒10, ‒20, ‒30, ‒40, and ‒50.
- Lila begins riding at 0 and pedals forward to 10.
- From 10, she pedals backward to ‒10.
- From ‒10, Lila rides forward to 20 and then backward to ‒20. She continues this pattern until she reaches ‒50. Then Lila rides forward to 0 and stops.

Answer Key 600 feet per day

Bonus Box answer: 70 and ‒70

Helpful Hints
Share this information when students get stuck to help put them back on the path to correctly solving the problem.

Hint 1 Draw a picture or diagram showing the path marked as described. Keep a list of each segment traveled and then add them.

Hint 2 Write an equation for each segment Lila travels. Remember that the distance between two points is the absolute value of the difference of the points. Use subtraction to determine the length of each segment. For example, 10 – (‒10) = 20.

Hint 3 Remember that linear distances are expressed as positive numbers.

One-Wheeled Wanderings

POW! #31

Lila wanted to be in the circus. First, she learned to juggle. Then she begged her mom for a unicycle. "OK," said her mom, after much pestering from Lila. "But they are very hard to ride."

Lila practiced every day on a 100-foot path. She didn't number her path from 0 to 100 though. Since unicycles can be pedaled both forward and backward, she marked the starting point (0) in the middle. Then, to the right of 0, Lila numbered the intervals 10, 20, 30, 40, and 50. To the left of 0, she wrote -10, -20, -30, -40, and -50.

Every day Lila started at 0 and pedaled forward to 10 and backward to -10. From there she rode forward to 20 and back ward to -20. Lila continued riding forward and backward until she reached -50. From there she pedaled forward to 0 and stopped.

"See, Mom?" Lila said. "I'm almost ready for the circus!"

"True," replied her math-loving mom. "But figure this out before you run off to join. What is the total daily distance you travel on your unicycle?"

Now It's Your Turn
Figure out how many feet Lila rode each day.

Bonus Box: To what number would Lila have to extend her number line so that she traveled an extra 520 feet each day?

The Three Little Fences

Finding the area of squares, rectangles, and circles

Problem-solving strategies

students could use:

- draw a diagram
- choose the correct operation
- guess and check
- make a list, table, or chart

Math skills

students will use:

- apply formulas
- relate perimeter and circumference
- relate area and perimeter
- find the area of squares, rectangles, and circles
- measure with customary units
- know the attributes of plane figures
- round decimals to the nearest tenth

Restating the problem: Each of the three little pigs builds a fence with a 64-foot perimeter around his yard. The fences all have different shapes and enclose different amounts of area. How much area does each fence enclose?

Important information found in the problem:
- Pig 1 builds a rectangular fence. Pig 2 builds a square fence. Pig 3 builds a circular fence.
- Each fence is built using one-foot segments that are either straight or curved.
- Each fence has a perimeter of 64 feet.
- Each fenced yard has a different area.
- The rectangular fence must be as large as possible without having four equal sides.

Answer Key

	Dimensions	Area	Relative Size
Pig 1 Rectangular Fence	L = 17 ft. W = 15 ft.	255 ft.^{2}	Smallest
Pig 2 Square Fence	Side = 16 ft.	256 ft.^{2}	Middle
Pig 3 Circular Fence	Diameter ≈ 20.4 ft. Radius ≈ 10.2 ft.	≈ 326.7 ft.^{2}	Largest

Bonus Box answer: Answers may vary.

Helpful Hints

Share this information when students get stuck to help put them back on the path to correctly solving the problem.

Hint 1 Find the largest possible rectangle by drawing a diagram and guessing and checking the length of the rectangle's sides. Or make a list of all possible combinations of length and width that equal a perimeter of 64 feet.

Hint 2 Use the formula side = p ÷ 4 to find the length of the square's sides.

Hint 3 Find the radius of the circular fence. Use the formula r = c ÷ (2π).

Hint 4 Round the answer for radius and area to the nearest tenth.

Hint 5 Use the following formulas to find the area of each yard:
- Area of a rectangle = length x width
- Area of a square = side^2
- Area of a circle = π x radius^2

The Three Little Fences

Once upon a time, there were three little pigs. Think you've heard this story before? Then let's fast-forward to the present. The three little pigs have rebuilt their homes and purchased fierce guard dogs to keep wolves away. However, each pig needs to build a fence around his yard to keep the dogs in.

"I'll build a rectangular fence," says Pig 1. "Then my dog can run back and forth and keep an eye out for wolves."

"I'll build a square fence," says Pig 2. "Then my dog can run the same distance from one corner to the next."

"I'll build a circular fence," says Pig 3. "Then a wolf won't be able to hide in a corner."

So off to the hardware store they go to buy fencing. The fencing comes in 1-foot segments—straight pieces for rectangular and square fences and curved pieces for round fences. Each pig buys 64 one-foot segments and goes home to build his fence.

All 3 fences—square, rectangular, and circular—have two things in common. They all keep wolves out, and they all have a perimeter of 64 feet. But when it's time to plant a garden, the pigs discover that their different fences give them different-sized yards. One pig discovers that he now has the smallest fenced yard, while another pig brags about having the largest. The third pig looks puzzled. "We all bought the same amount of fencing," he says. "Why don't we have yards with the same area?"

Now It's Your Turn

Help the pigs find the area of each yard. Then rank the yards from largest to smallest. Remember that each yard must have a perimeter of 64 feet. Design the rectangular yard to be as large as possible without having 4 equal sides.

Bonus Box: Choose another fairy tale or nursery rhyme and write a math problem that uses the characters and situation of that story. Be sure to include the answer to the problem.

Show Me the Money!

Finding a fractional part of a number and converting it to a percent

Problem-solving strategies

students could use:

- make a list, table, or chart
- find a pattern
- choose the correct operation
- write an equation
- solve a simpler problem

Math skills

students will use:

- find a fractional part of a number
- convert fractions to decimals and decimals to percents
- find a percent of a number
- round decimals to the nearest cent
- use ratios and proportions

Ima Brainiac

Restating the problem: Ima Brainiac wins $1,000,000.00 on a game show but must receive it in five payments. The first payment is $\frac{1}{3}$ of $1,000,000.00. Each of the four remaining payments is half the amount of the previous one. When will Ima receive 50% of her money? 60%? What percent of the total prize money will she have after the five payments?

Important information found in the problem:
- Ima Brainiac wins $1,000,000.00 on a game show.
- The check for the prize money bounces, and the producer offers Ima a new payment plan.
- Today Ima receives $\frac{1}{3}$ of $1,000,000.00
- One year from now, Ima receives $\frac{1}{6}$ of $1,000,000.00
- Two years from now, Ima receives $\frac{1}{12}$ of $1,000,000.00
- Three years from now, Ima receives $\frac{1}{24}$ of $1,000,000.00
- Four years from now, Ima receives $\frac{1}{48}$ of $1,000,000.00, her final payment.

Answer Key One year from now, Ima will have 50% ($500,000.00) of her money. Three years from now, she will have more than 60% ($625,000.00). After the fifth payment, Ima will have about 65% of the total prize money ($645,833.33).

Bonus Box answer: Ima would never get the full $1,000,000.00 according to this pattern. Her total winnings would be about 67% ($666,666.03) at the end of 20 years.

Helpful Hints

Share this information when students get stuck to help put them back on the path to correctly solving the problem.

Hint 1 The word *of* signals a multiplication operation. For example, to find $\frac{1}{3}$ of $1,000,000.00, multiply $\frac{1}{3}$ times $1,000,000.00. Or since the numerator of the fraction is 1, divide $1,000,000.00 by the denominator to find that fractional part of $1,000,000.00.

Hint 2 Change a fraction to a percent by using a proportion. For example, $\frac{1}{3} = x/1,000,000$. Multiply the cross products. Then solve to find the value of the variable.

Hint 3 Make a table showing each payment's date, the fraction of the total, the amount of money, and the percent of $1,000,000.00.

Hint 4 When dividing money, round to the nearest cent.

Hint 5 Look for a pattern in the amount of money Ima receives with each payment. (*The amount decreases by half.*)

Hint 6 Solve a simpler problem, using $100.00 instead of $1,000,000.00. This makes each percent equal to a dollar amount. For example, 50% is $50.00.

Show Me the Money!

Ima Brainiac is not sorry she flew to Los Angeles to be a contestant on a game show. And she's definitely not sorry she won the grand prize of $1,000,000.00! She *is* sorry, however, that she didn't make sure the game show producer had $1,000,000.00 in the bank before she started spending her prize money.

"The check bounced," she yelled when she got the show's producer on the phone.

"I know," he said. "We haven't been getting good ratings lately. But don't worry, Ima. We'll make things right. Just give us a little more time."

"I guess I don't have much choice," said Ima. "But I'll need some cash right away, because I just spent the weekend at the mall."

"Here's what we'll do," the producer said. "We'll give you $\frac{1}{3}$ of the money right now. One year later, you will receive $\frac{1}{6}$ of the money. In 2 years, you'll get $\frac{1}{12}$ and in 3 years, you can have $\frac{1}{24}$. The fifth and final payment will be $\frac{1}{48}$ of a million."

Ima wasn't a Brainiac for nothing. She quickly calculated how long it would take her to get 50% and then 60% of her prize money. Then Ima figured out the total amount of money she would receive in 5 years. She wasn't too happy about the answers.

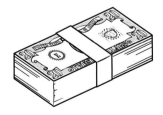  

Now It's Your Turn
If Ima receives her first payment today, when will she have at least 50% of her money? When will she have 60%? What percent of $1,000,000.00 will she have after all 5 payments have been made?

Bonus Box: If this pattern of payment continued for the next 20 years, would Ima get the full $1,000,000.00? What percent of the total prize money would she have after 20 years?

Chances Are...

Comparing the likelihood of four events

Teacher Page

Problem-solving strategies

students could use:

- make a list, table, or chart
- choose the correct operation

Math skills

students will use:

- determine the probability of events
- express probability as a ratio
- convert fractions to decimals and percents
- write fractions in simplest form
- compare fractions and percents
- convert weeks to days

Restating the problem: Jo Jones loves to calculate probability. She makes observations about four school events. Which of the four events is most likely to occur? Least likely?

Important information found in the problem:

- To join the Chances-Are Probability Club, prospective members must determine which of four events are most likely and least likely to occur.
- The four events:
  In P.E. class, students run laps for ten minutes during each 42-minute period.
  The Spanish teacher gives homework only on Tuesdays and Thursdays.
  The science teacher schedules nine periods of labs for every six weeks of school.
  The math teacher allows students to use calculators on three out of every 11 problems.
- Jo asks her classmates to figure out which events are most likely and least likely to occur.

Answer Key The probability of running laps is $^5/_{21}$ or 24%; having Spanish homework, $^2/_5$ or 40%; having a science lab, $^3/_{10}$ or 30%; using a calculator, $^3/_{11}$ or 27%. The most likely event is being assigned Spanish homework; the least likely event is running laps in P.E.

Bonus Box answer: Answers will vary but should be arranged in a chart, such as the one shown.

Event	Time	Fraction	Decimal	Percent
sleeping	8 hr.	$\frac{1}{3}$	0.33	33%
going to school	7 hr.	$\frac{7}{24}$	0.29	29%
doing homework	1 hr.	$\frac{1}{24}$	0.04	4%
eating	1 hr.	$\frac{1}{24}$	0.04	4%
talking on the phone	45 min.	$\frac{1}{32}$	0.03	3%
watching TV	2 hr.	$\frac{1}{12}$	0.08	8%
playing with friends	30 min.	$\frac{1}{48}$	0.02	2%

Helpful Hints

Share this information when students get stuck to help put them back on the path to correctly solving the problem.

Hint 1 Make a chart with five columns: Event, Time, Fraction, Decimal, Percent. Write a fraction showing the probability of each event. Then complete the chart by writing each fraction as a decimal and each decimal as a percent.

Hint 2 The numerator of each fraction tells how many favorable outcomes there are. The denominator tells the number of possible outcomes. For example, the number of days Spanish homework is given *(2)* is the numerator. The number of days homework could be given *(5)* is the denominator.

Hint 3 Be sure that the units in each fraction match. Science labs are held nine days out of six weeks. Convert six weeks into 30 days. Then write the probability as a fraction $^9/_{30}$, which can be reduced to $^3/_{10}$.

Hint 4 It is easier to compare fractions after they have been converted to decimals and percents. To do this, divide the numerator by the denominator to get a decimal. Round each decimal to the nearest hundredth if necessary. Next, multiply the decimal by 100 to get the percent. Then compare the percents to identify the most likely and least likely events.

Chances Are...

POW!
#34

Most kids make hundreds of decisions every day, beginning with which cereal to eat and which pair of shoes to wear.

Josephine Jones has absolutely no interest in those types of decisions. To Jo Jones, the only good decisions are those that can be answered mathematically. For example, ask her what the chances are that her bowl of cereal will contain exactly 3 star-shaped marshmallows, and she'll grow quite interested! In fact, she'll quickly calculate the probability, basing it on a ratio of 1 marshmallow star to 62 corn nuggets.

One day at school, Jo announced that she was starting the Chances-Are Probability Club. Anyone who could solve her puzzle correctly could join.

Jo presented 4 events based upon her own observations.

1. In P.E., students run laps for 10 minutes during each 42-minute class.
2. The Spanish teacher gives homework only on Tuesdays and Thursdays.
3. The science teacher schedules 9 periods of labs for every 6 weeks of school.
4. The math teacher allows students to use calculators on 3 out of every 11 problems.

Jo told her classmates that to join the club, they'd have to figure out which of the 4 events are most likely and least likely to occur.

Now It's Your Turn

Give the probability of all 4 events. List each probability in 2 forms: as a fraction written in simplest form and as a percent. Then identify which event is most likely and least likely to occur.

Bonus Box: Think about your average weekday. How much time each day would you estimate that you spend sleeping? Going to school? Doing homework? Eating? Talking on the phone? Watching TV? Playing with friends? Make a chart showing the estimated time spent on each activity. Then determine the fraction, decimal, and percent that represent the time spent on that activity during an average 24-hour day.

Soup's On!

Finding the fractional parts of a number

Problem-solving strategies

students could use:
- work backward
- guess and check
- act it out

Math skills

students will use:
- find the fractional part of a number
- use ratios and proportions
- cross multiply
- find a common denominator

Restating the problem: One by one, three chefs remove bones from a giant bag to make soup. In the end, Dixie Dog gets the leftovers. How many bones were in the bag at first? How many bones did each chef use?

Important information found in the problem:
- Three chefs—Pierre, Marie, and Antoine—take turns using bones to make soup.
- Pierre, the first chef, used one-fifth of the bones.
- Marie, the second chef, used one-half of the remaining bones.
- Antoine, the third chef, used two-thirds of the remaining bones.
- Antoine had four bones left over.

(Answer Key) Total bones = 30. Pierre used 6; Marie used 12; Antoine used 8.

Bonus Box answer: Answers may vary.

Helpful Hints

Share this information when students get stuck to help put them back on the path to correctly solving the problem.

Hint 1 Starting with Antoine, work backward to solve this problem.

Hint 2 If Antoine used two-thirds of the bones, one-third *(4 bones)* was left for Dixie. Write a proportion *($4/x = 1/3$)* and cross multiply to find out how many bones Antoine had to start with *(12)*.

Hint 3 Antoine received half the bones that Marie started with. If Antoine started with 12 bones (see hint 2), then Marie had twice that many *(24)* to start with.

Hint 4 If Pierre used one-fifth of the bones, then he had four-fifths left over to give Marie. If Marie started with 24 bones (see hint 3), which was four-fifths of the bones left, write a proportion *($24/x = 4/5$)* and cross multiply to find out how many bones there were to start with *(30)*.

Hint 5 Find the common denominator of the fractions to get a clue about the total number of bones in the bag.

Hint 6 Using manipulatives to represent the bones, guess and check to arrive at the answer.

Soup's On!

This is a story about three chefs and a little dog. Each of the chefs would love to tell you what happened, but I'd rather have you hear the story from the happiest creature at the café, Dixie Dog.

"Okay," said Dixie, "here's how it happened. The first chef, Pierre, arrived this morning to make soup. He tore open a giant bag of bones. Mmm, I love bones. They taste so good, I wish I had..."

"Dixie Dog! Get on with the story!"

"Right. After counting the bones, Pierre used $\frac{1}{5}$ of them to start his soup. He left after lunch and Chef Marie arrived to make a different soup for dinner. She saw how many bones were left in the bag and put $\frac{1}{2}$ of them in her soup. She could have saved one for me, but..."

"Let's stick to the story, Dixie."

"Of course. After Marie left, Chef Antoine arrived. He counted the bones and put $\frac{2}{3}$ of what remained in his soup. That left 4 bones...and guess what! He gave them to me!"

"Okay, Dixie Dog. Go back to your bones. We'll do the math without you."

Now It's Your Turn
How many bones were in the bag originally? How many bones did each chef use?

Bonus Box: Write a problem about a similar situation. Be sure to include the answer.

Who Wants Pizza?

Using the digits 1–5 to make the greatest and least possible fractions

Problem-solving strategies

students could use:

- guess and check
- make a list, table, or chart
- find a pattern
- draw a picture or diagram

Math skills

students will use:

- compare and order fractions
- subtract fractions with unlike denominators
- simplify fractions
- measure with tools such as a compass, protractor, and ruler
- convert fractions to degrees
- construct a circle graph
- represent fractions in pictorial form

Restating the problem: Jonathan wants to eat as little of his sister's hot-dog-and-bean casserole and as much pizza as possible. To accomplish his goal, he must use each digit 1–5 once to write the two fractions that have the greatest difference. What are the fractions?

Important information found in the problem:

- Jonathan wants to eat as little casserole and as much pizza as possible.
- His father offers a mathematical solution. Using the digits 1–5 once each, find the two fractions that have the greatest difference.
- The smaller fraction will be Jonathan's share of the casserole and the larger fraction his share of the pizza.
- Improper fractions may not be used.
- If Jonathan finds the two fractions having the greatest difference, he will get ice cream for dessert.

Answer Key The two fractions with the greatest difference are $4/5$ and $1/32$. The difference is $123/160$.

Bonus Box answer:

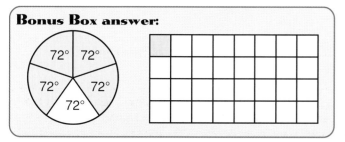

Helpful Hints

Share this information when students get stuck to help put them back on the path to correctly solving the problem.

Hint 1 Keep a list or chart showing which pairs of fractions have been tried and what their differences are.

Hint 2 Look for patterns. Which makes a fraction larger: increasing the numerator or the denominator? Which of these makes a fraction smaller? Which gives bigger differences, starting with the smallest possible number or the greatest possible number?

Hint 3 List the greatest fractions possible. Then use the remaining digits to show the smallest fraction to go with each. Repeat for the smallest fractions. For example, the least possible fraction is $1/54$. Use the remaining digits, 2 and 3, to make the greatest fraction possible, $2/3$.

Hint 4 Subtract each fraction pair to find the greatest difference.

Who Wants Pizza?

A little knowledge can be a dangerous thing. So why didn't anyone but Jonathan remember that when his sister, Ali, said she wanted to learn how to cook?

"Great idea!" said Mom.

"Wonderful!" agreed Pop.

"Can I eat at Grandma's?" Jonathan asked hopefully.

After a few lessons, Ali was ready to make her first meal: a hot-dog-and-baked-bean casserole. She mixed onions, hot dogs, and baked beans.

Then she thought, "This isn't going to taste very interesting. Maybe I should add some other kinds of beans." So in went a can of lima beans, plus a can of string beans. And, to top it off, in went a bag of jelly beans!

As Ali put the colorful casserole in the oven, Pop caught a glimpse of it. He quickly ordered a pizza.

At dinnertime, both the bean casserole and the pizza were served.

"How colorful!" exclaimed Mom.

"How creative!" complimented Pop.

"How disgusting!" grumbled Jonathan. "I won't eat that casserole!"

"Sure you will," encouraged Pop. "It will give you practice in math."

"How?" asked Jonathan.

Pop wrote the numbers 1, 2, 3, 4, and 5 on a napkin. "Use all 5 digits 1 time each to make 2 fractions," he told Jonathan. "The smaller fraction will represent how much of Ali's casserole you will eat and the larger fraction how much pizza you will eat. And if you find the fraction pair that has the greatest possible difference, you can even have ice cream for dessert!"

Now It's Your Turn

**Use the digits 1–5 once each to write 2 fractions that have the greatest difference.
Do not use improper fractions. List both fractions and find their difference.**

Bonus Box: Show your answers in a drawing. Make a circle to represent the pizza and a rectangle to represent the casserole. Use measuring tools—such as a compass, a protractor, and a ruler—to divide the pizza and casserole into the number of pieces represented by the denominators. Then color the number of pieces Jonathan will eat of each food.

Something's Fishy!

Teacher Page

Finding a container with sufficient volume to hold seven fish

Problem-solving strategies

students could use:
- choose the correct operation
- write an equation

Math skills

students will use:
- decide whether an answer is reasonable
- convert decimals and fractions
- convert customary units
- use a formula to find volume of rectangular prisms
- compare decimals
- round decimals to the nearest tenth
- interpret remainder

Restating the problem: Darrell orders an aquarium and some tropical fish, but the fish arrive without the aquarium. He must decide which of three containers will make the best temporary home for his fish. Which one should he choose?

Important information found in the problem:
- Darrell knows that he needs a gallon of water for each inch of fish length.
- He ordered three neon tetras (1 inch each), two cardinal tetras ($1\frac{1}{2}$ inches each), one diamond tetra (2 inches), and one white tip shark catfish (2.5 inches).
- His parents offer him a choice of three vases from their flower shop. All are rectangular prisms.
- Vase 1 is a 13-inch cube. Vase 2 is 14 inches long, 8 inches wide, and 24 inches high. Vase 3 is 12 inches long, 12 inches wide, and 17 inches high.
- Useful formulas for this problem include the following: volume of a cube ($V = s^3$) and volume of a rectangular prism ($V = l \times w \times h$).
- One gallon equals 231 in.^{3}.

Answer Key Vase 1: V = 2,197 in.^{3} (holds about 9.5 gal.); Vase 2: V = 2,688 in.^{3} (holds about 11.6 gal.); Vase 3: V = 2,448 in.^{3} (holds about 10.6 gal.). Vase 3 is the best choice because the seven fish would require 2,425.5 in.^{3} (10.5 gal.).

Bonus Box answer: Darrell's room would hold about 3,890 two-inch diamond tetras.

Helpful Hints

Share this information when students get stuck to help put them back on the path to correctly solving the problem.

Hint 1 — Some students may need to visualize the vases by sketching and labeling them with dimensions.

Hint 2 — To find the volume of vase 1, multiply 13" x 13" x 13". For vase 2, multiply 14" x 8" x 24". For vase 3, multiply 12" x 12" x 17".

Hint 3 — The sum of the lengths of the fish is 10.5 in., which means Darrell needs at least 10.5 gal. of water. Multiply 10.5 gal. by 231 in.^{3} per gallon. The aquarium's volume must be at least 2,425.5 in.^{3}.

Hint 4 — Vase 1 has a volume of 2,197 in.^{3}. Vase 2 has a volume of 2,688 in.^{3}. Vase 3 has a volume of 2,448 in.^{3}.

Something's Fishy!

When the special delivery truck pulled up to his house, Darrell couldn't contain his excitement. Here at last was his birthday present, a custom-built aquarium along with the tropical fish he'd selected.

But the package he was handed was much too small to contain his tank. Sure enough, as the letter inside explained, the aquarium would not arrive until next week. Meanwhile, here were the fish.

"That's impossible!" Darrell protested. "I can't have the fish until I have a place to put them!"

He called his parents at their flower shop.

His dad tried to reassure him. "Don't worry, Darrell. We have lots of big glass vases here that you can use," he said.

"But you don't understand. It can't be just any vase. It has to be the right size, one that allows 1 gallon of water per inch of fish."

"Son," his Dad replied, "make a list of each fish and its size. We'll bring our biggest vases home at lunch."

Darrell listed the fish: 3 neon tetras (1 inch each), 2 cardinal tetras ($1\frac{1}{2}$ inches each), 1 diamond tetra (2 inches), and 1 white tip shark catfish (2.5 inches).

His parents brought him 3 vases, all rectangular prisms. Vase 1 was a 13-inch cube. Vase 2 was 14 inches long, 8 inches wide, and 24 inches high. Vase 3 was 12 inches long, 12 inches wide, and 17 inches high.

Darrell found the volume of each vase using the formula volume = length x width x height. His mom told him there are 231 cubic inches in 1 gallon. That was all he needed to pick the vase that came closest to what he needed without being too small.

Now It's Your Turn

Calculate the number of cubic inches of space Darrell's fish need and the volume of each vase. Then figure out which of the three vases is the best choice. Remember: The vase should come as close as possible to the exact number without being too small.

Bonus Box: That night, Darrell dreamed that his bedroom had turned into an aquarium full of fish. If his bedroom measures 13' x 10' x 8' and he sticks to the rule of 1 gallon of water per inch of fish, how many 2-inch diamond tetras would fit in his room? (Hint: Turn feet into inches before finding the volume so you can turn cubic inches into gallons.)

School Shopping Spree

Finding combinations to equal exact amounts

Problem-solving strategies

students could use:

- work backward
- guess and check
- make a list, table, or chart

Math skills

students will use:

- draw conclusions
- make and test predictions
- use number sense
- multiply units of currency

Restating the problem: A math teacher is given $100.00 to purchase abacuses, compasses, and chalk. She must buy the right combination of supplies so that she spends exactly $100.00 on 100 items. What combination of the three items can she buy?

Important information found in the problem:
- The school has an extra $100.00.
- The teacher must spend exactly $100.00 on supplies.
- The teacher must buy exactly 100 items.
- She must buy at least one of each of the three items (abacus, compass, chalk).
- An abacus costs $10.00.
- A compass costs $1.00.
- A piece of chalk costs $0.50.

Answer Key

	Abacuses	Compasses	Chalk
Answer 1	2 ($20.00)	62 ($62.00)	36 ($18.00)
Answer 2	3 ($30.00)	43 ($43.00)	54 ($27.00)
Answer 3	4 ($40.00)	24 ($24.00)	72 ($36.00)
Answer 4	5 ($50.00)	5 ($5.00)	90 ($45.00)

Bonus Box answer: 5 calculators

Helpful Hints

Share this information when students get stuck to help put them back on the path to correctly solving the problem.

Hint 1 The number of chalk sticks must be even.

Hint 2 Make a table showing the number and cost of the abacuses, the number and cost of the compasses, and the number and cost of the chalk.

Hint 3 Try different combinations of items.

School Shopping Spree

Who ever heard of a school having too much money? That's certainly never happened in our lifetime. But legend has it that about a hundred years ago in a small village, a school principal once had $100.00 left over after all the bills were paid. Rather than give it back to the school board, the principal decided to send the school's best math teacher to town to spend it immediately.

"Just get abacuses, compasses, and chalk," said the principal. "However, you must follow these rules: Spend exactly $100.00—not a penny more or a penny less. Buy exactly 100 items. Buy at least one of each item."

The teacher jumped in her wagon and drove to town. At the store, she discovered that an abacus cost $10.00, a compass cost $1.00, and a stick of chalk cost $0.50.

"Wow," she thought, "this is going to be harder than I thought. I have to spend exactly $100.00 and buy exactly 100 items. What shall I do?"

Now It's Your Turn

What combination of abacuses, compasses, and chalk should the teacher buy? Remember, the solution must add up two different ways. The total amount spent must equal $100.00 and the teacher must purchase 100 items.

Bonus Box: What is the maximum number of abacuses the teacher can buy?

Make Room for Magic

Scaling down objects to fit in a space

Problem-solving strategies

students could use:

- draw a picture or diagram
- choose the correct operation
- guess and check
- make a list, table, or chart
- act it out

Math skills

students will use:

- convert customary units of measurement
- construct similar solid figures
- use proportion and scale
- develop an understanding of spatial relationships
- compare measurements
- calculate and diameter
- use manipulatives

Restating the problem: Merwyn is a magnificent magician but a terrible packer. He needs to shrink his magic props so that everything will fit in his trunk. What is the least amount he must shrink each prop?

Important information found in the problem:

- Merwyn needs to shrink four props so they will all fit in his trunk.
- The trunk measures 12 inches high, six inches wide, and 18 inches long.
- Merwyn wants to use the smallest shrink factor possible for each prop.
- The crystal ball has an 18-inch diameter.
- The disappearing tube measures one foot in diameter and is 32 inches long.
- The rabbit cage is a two-foot cube.
- The box for sawing ladies in half is 7½ feet long, 20 inches tall, and 30 inches wide.

Answer Key

Prop	Shrink Factor	New Dimensions Length	New Dimensions Width/Diameter	New Dimensions Height
Crystal Ball	3		6 in.	
Disappearing Tube	4	8 in.	3 in.	
Rabbit Cage	4	6 in.	6 in.	6 in.
Sawing Box	5	18 in.	6 in.	4 in.

Bonus Box answer: shrink factor—3; new measurements—4 in. tall, 3 in. diameter

Helpful Hints

Share this information when students get stuck to help put them back on the path to correctly solving the problem.

Hint 1 Change all measurements to inches.

Hint 2 Sketch the trunk and each prop. Label each sketch with the appropriate dimensions.

Hint 3 Make a half model of the trunk from centimeter graph paper, using a scale of 1 cm = 1 inch as shown. As each prop is reduced in size, lightly shade in an area on the graph paper to represent its placement in the trunk.

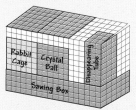

Hint 4 The shrink factor is the number by which each dimension will be divided to reduce (scale down) the object's size and make it fit in the trunk with the other props. It is a common factor of the object's dimensions.

Hint 5 To find the new size of each prop, write a proportion. Use the original length, width, or diameter as the numerator and the shrink factor as the denominator. For the equivalent part of the proportion, use a variable such as *x* for the numerator and the number 1 for the denominator. Cross multiply to solve. Repeat for each dimension.

Make Room for Magic

POW!
#39

Merwyn was a magnificent magician. He made rabbits appear, sawed ladies in half, read the future in a crystal ball, and made things vanish into thin air. However, the magnificent Merwyn had one problem—he was a terrible packer. No matter how hard he tried, Merwyn always had one item that wouldn't fit in his trunk.

Merwyn mulled over his packing problem and decided he'd call the Magicians' Hotline. "Use your magic powers, Merwyn, and put a shrinking spell on your props so they will fit in your trunk."

Merwyn measured his trunk—12 inches tall, 6 inches wide, and 18 inches long. The props Merwyn needed to pack in the trunk measured as follows:

- crystal ball = 18-inch diameter
- disappearing tube = 1-foot diameter and 32 inches long
- cage for rabbits = 2-foot cube
- box for sawing ladies in half = $7\frac{1}{2}$ feet long, 20 inches tall, and 30 inches wide

Before Merwyn could use his magic powers, however, he needed to know what shrink factor to use for each item so that all 4 props would fit in the trunk.

Now It's Your Turn

Determine the shrink factor Merwyn needs to use for each prop so all of the items will fit in his trunk. Include the new measurements in your answer. Remember: Shrink each prop the least amount necessary.

Bonus Box: Suppose that Merwyn decided to add his hat, which measured 12 inches tall and had a 9-inch diameter, to his trunk of props. Determine the hat's shrink factor and new measurements.

or Pete's Sake!

Counting to ten using only fours

Problem-solving strategies
students could use:
- work backward
- guess and check
- logical reasoning

Math skills
students will use:
- write equations
- use basic facts
- use number sense
- write fractions
- use correct order of operations
- use parentheses and brackets

Restating the problem: Pete is trying to convince his teacher that he needs only fours to count to ten. How can Pete count to ten using only fours?

Important information found in the problem:
- Pete wrote ten equations.
- Each equation used only four fours.
- Pete used fractions.
- Pete used basic operations ($+$, $-$, $\times$, $\div$).
- Pete used parentheses and brackets.
- $^{44}/_{44} = 1$
- $^4/_4 + {^4}/_4 = 2$
- $[(4 \times 4) - 4] \div 4 = 3$

Answer Key Written explanations will vary.
Possible answers include the following:

$^{44}/_{44} = 1$	$(4 + 4) \div 4 + 4 = 6$
$^4/_4 + {^4}/_4 = 2$	$4 - (4 \div 4) + 4 = 7$
$[(4 \times 4) - 4] \div 4 = 3$	$(4 \times 4) \div 4 + 4 = 8$
$(4 - 4) \times 4 + 4 = 4$	$(4 \div 4) + 4 + 4 = 9$
$[(4 \times 4) + 4] \div 4 = 5$	$(44 - 4) \div 4 = 10$

Bonus Box answer:
$4 - (4 \div 4) + 4 + 4 = 11$
$(4 \times 4) \div 4 + 4 + 4 = 12$
$(4 + 4) + 4 + {^{44}}/_{44} = 13$
$(44 - 4) \div 4 + 4 = 14$
$(4 \times 4) - (4 \div 4) = 15$

Helpful Hints
Share this information when students get stuck to help put them back on the path to correctly solving the problem.

Hint 1 The *order of operations* is a set of rules that tells you the order in which to compute a problem.

1. Compute inside the parentheses first; then compute inside the brackets.
2. Compute exponents.
3. Multiply or divide in order from left to right.
4. Add or subtract in order from left to right.

Hint 2 Use this silly sentence to help students remember the order of operations:

Please **e**xcuse **m**y **d**ear **A**unt **S**ally.
(**p**arentheses, **e**xponents, **m**ultiplication, **d**ivision, **a**ddition, **s**ubtraction)

Hint 3 Inform students that not every step in the order of operations is used in every problem. For example, only some of the ten equations in the word problem's answer contain brackets and none of the equations contain exponents.

For Pete's Sake!

Say hello to Pete.

Pete loves the number 4. Perhaps it's because he was born at 4:44 A.M. on April 4. Pete is also the fourth child in his family.

Pete is such a smart young man that when he entered school, he began in the fourth grade!

On the first day of school when Pete's teacher introduced the math lesson, Pete raised his hand and said, "I don't see any reason to learn numbers. The number 4 is the only one I need!" Pete could be quite stubborn.

Pete's teacher did all she could to convince him that he needed to learn all of the numbers. How else would he ever count to 10?

Luckily for Pete, he had a plan. He told his teacher that he could count to 10 using only 4s. He then went to the chalkboard and wrote the following 3 equations:

$$\frac{44}{44} = 1$$

$$\frac{4}{4} + \frac{4}{4} = 2$$

$$[(4 \times 4) - 4] \div 4 = 3$$

Using the basic arithmetic operations (+, −, x, ÷) and exactly four 4s each time, Pete proceeded to count to 10!

Now It's Your Turn

Help Pete finish writing the numbers 1–10. Remember, exactly four 4s are used for each equation. You'll likely think of more than one way to write a number. If so, list each one.

Bonus Box: A classmate asked Pete to extend his writing to include the numbers 11–15. Help Pete do this. You can use more than four 4s.

More great math books from *The Mailbox*®

TEC849. The Best of *The Mailbox*® Math • Grades 4–6
TEC883. The Best of *Teacher's Helper*® Math • Book 1 • Grades 4–5
TEC3213. The Best of *Teacher's Helper*® Math • Book 2 • Grades 4–5

Managing Editor: Peggy W. Hambright

Editor at Large: Diane Badden

Staff Editors: Cayce Guiliano, Christa New

Writer: Abby Karp

Copy Editors: Sylvan Allen, Karen Brewer Grossman, Karen L. Huffman, Amy Kirtley-Hill, Debbie Shoffner

Cover Artist: Barry Slate

Art Coordinator: Nick Greenwood

Artists: Pam Crane, Nick Greenwood, Ivy L. Koonce, Sheila Krill, Clint Moore, Greg D. Rieves, Rebecca Saunders, Barry Slate, Stuart Smith, Donna K. Teal

Typesetters: Lynette Dickerson, Mark Rainey

President, The Mailbox Book Company™: Joseph C. Bucci

Director of Book Planning and Development: Chris Poindexter

Book Development Managers: Elizabeth H. Lindsay, Thad McLaurin, Susan Walker

Curriculum Director: Karen P. Shelton

Traffic Manager: Lisa K. Pitts

Librarian: Dorothy C. McKinney

Editorial and Freelance Management: Karen A. Brudnak

Editorial Training: Irving P. Crump

Editorial Assistants: Hope Rodgers, Jan E. Witcher

Manufactured in the United States
10 9 8 7 6 5 4 3 2 1